HANS KÜNG

*Director of the Institute for Ecumenical Studies
at the University of Tübingen*

The Changing Church

Reflections on the Progress of the Second Vatican Council

Translated by CECILY HASTINGS
WILLIAM GLEN-DOEPEL
H. R. BRONK

SHEED AND WARD

LONDON   MELBOURNE

NEW YORK

FIRST PUBLISHED 1965
SHEED AND WARD LTD
33 MAIDEN LANE
LONDON W.C.2
AND
SHEED AND WARD PTY LTD
28 BOURKE STREET
MELBOURNE

NIHIL OBSTAT: JOANNES M. T. BARTON, S.T.D., L.S.S.
CENSOR DEPUTATUS

IMPRIMATUR: PATRITIUS CASEY, VIC. GEN.

WESTMONASTERII, DIE 18 MARCH 1965

The Nihil obstat *and* Imprimatur *are a declaration that a book
or pamphlet is considered to be free from doctrinal or moral error.
It is not implied that those who have granted the* Nihil obstat *and*
Imprimatur *agree with the contents, opinions or statements expressed.*

This book is set in 12 pt. Linotype Baskerville

*Made and printed in Great Britain by
William Clowes and Sons, Limited, London and Beccles*

CONTENTS

PUBLISHER'S NOTE

The studies which are combined in this book were originally published as running commentaries on the life of the Church as it unfolds in the present crucial phase of crisis, change and vital renewal. They are here presented almost wholly unaltered, since it was felt that their historicity is an essential element in their continuing relevance.

WHY POPE JOHN WAS GREAT

JOHN XXIII was not what the world would call a great speaker or a great diplomat, a great linguist, a great jurist or a great scholar. In fact, with all his remarkable intuitive intelligence, he was not really what Church history would call a great theologian. And yet if I were asked and—without anticipating the verdict of history—were to answer, simply and spontaneously, the question, "Who is the greatest pope of this century?", I should unhesitatingly reply, "John XXIII". And if someone were to point out to me all the great things that John XXIII was not—but who would be interested since Pope John did just this himself in his coronation address?—then I would say that ultimately none of that matters when compared with the one thing in which he was great: *service*. And in this he has behind him the word of another, who puts his greatness beyond dispute: "If any one would be first, he must be last of all and servant of all."

And wasn't it this that made this pope so popular, indeed, so loved by countless millions both inside and outside the Catholic Church? This pope was not, like so many of his predecessors, wondered at, admired, or even feared. He was loved. Here was a man who, without pretentiousness whatever, simply did his job. He never considered himself as special; he disliked posed photographs in pious attitudes and made jokes about not being photogenic. And yet pictures of him were always attractive and often touching: this face without guile, humble, kind, lovable. John XXIII did not pretend to knowledge when he had none. He did not pretend that he wrote every official document ("I've read it!" he said once, with a chuckle, of his first encyclical). But whenever he spoke, his words, inspired by the Gospel, went straight to the heart. The Roman pomp which surrounded him, difficult to remove, he was totally indifferent to. He had little time for demonstrations of honour towards him. He did without the *sedia gestatoria* whenever he could and entered St Peter's on foot. In order to avoid an ovation as he came into the basilica he had the Apostles' Creed sung. He personally introduced concelebration in St Peter's. He loved to pray with the faithful in St Peter's Square at midday from his window, but always withdrew immediately in order to avoid any ovation.

THE EVANGELIST

What makes a man great in the eyes of other men was of no concern to John XXIII; but what makes a man great—according to the Gospel—in the eyes of God, was important to him. And it was this specifically evangelical quality which distinguished him from his great predecessors. Not only was he strictly opposed to all family politics and all nepotism. Not only did he, as the Bishop of Rome, concern himself in a new—or rather old— way about his own flock and his own clergy, visiting individual parishes in the suburbs himself. No, the chief thing was that, without making any fuss about it, he reminded us of old evangelical truths which, in Rome of all places, had been strangely forgotten. Who of his great predecessors had ever, as Pope, personally visited the poor, comforted the sick in hospital, sought out priests who had suffered a breakdown? Who had gone to the Roman state prison and, in a place which would severely test the greatest speakers, found the right words to say? Simply, he told the prisoners and criminals, who never dreamed of such a visit, that prisons had always affected him profoundly since his boyhood, because his own uncle had gone to gaol for poaching. The *Osservatore Romano,* which often suppressed the best thing in the Pope's speeches, replaced the word "uncle" with "relation"— apparently more in keeping with the dignity. of the Pope. . . .

Pope John never tried to appear an extraordinary man, or a saint in his own lifetime. If anyone had called him that he would certainly have laughed. He never stood on his dignity. During the Council he received a great national conference of bishops for which he had prepared an address in French, but the speech of greeting to him was in Latin. He therefore felt compelled to give his address in Latin also, but his translation from French to Latin was not altogether successful. He apologised, saying that he had not made any speeches in Latin since the time he taught church history at a seminary. Leaving the room he said to the bishops, "Oggi abbiamo fatto una brutta figura!" ("Today we cut a poor figure!") And that after *Veterum Sapientia* (the constitution in favour of church Latin, which a few Roman prelates had forced out of him).—"But I didn't write it myself!" So he was never too solemn about himself. As he once told a bishop, if he could not sleep for worry he would let "the Pope" say, "Angelo, don't take yourself so seriously!"

All men of good will always felt with this man that he did not want to be there for himself, but only for others. He did not want to force people, he wanted to convince through love. He did not want to instruct from on high; he wanted, from a deep understanding of the achievements and the needs of the modern world, to help as a brother. That could be heard in everything he said and particularly in his last encyclical *Pacem in Terris*, which, with its message of peace and justice, religious freedom, human rights and the brotherhood of all men, echoed round the world. John XXIII thus made the office of Peter within the Church, often elevated to an institution between heaven and earth, more human again and more lovable. Or rather, he tried to make the office of Peter, based on the Gospels, evangelical in a new way, according to the demands of the Gospel. That is why Pope John was so popular with the Evangelical Church. That is why he was a great pope.

FRIENDLY TO THE COMMUNISTS?

In the fundamental area of doctrine and ethics John XXIII never made the slightest concession to communism. On the contrary, he always demanded, in opposition to totalitarianism, respect for the dignity, the freedom, and the rights of the individual in state and society. But he was profoundly convinced that it is not sufficient to be simply "against" something. He saw the *positive* task of being responsible for *all* Christians—including those behind the Iron Curtain, whom we always praise in theory, but in practice are largely written off. Pope John was never ready to write them off.

The invitation of the spiritual representatives of the Russian Orthodox Church was a courageous decision. John XXIII, for a long time Apostolic Delegate in countries of the Orthodox persuasion, knew how important the attitude of the Russian Orthodox Church to the Council and its endeavours would be for the attitude of all the Orthodox churches. He knew that by far the largest part of the Eastern church—many, many millions—live within the sphere of Russian political influence. He wanted to help these millions of suffering Christians, Catholic and non-Catholic. Help and service were here, as always, uppermost in his mind, not strategy and politics. That is why he invited representatives of these Christians. It was certainly reasons of political opportunism which made the Soviet Government agree to the representatives attending the Council. For the Russian Orthodox Church itself, however, it was of the greatest importance to make contact for the first time in long decades with the Catholic Church at its heart, to listen, to observe, and to reply. Those who spoke to the Russian observers at the Council know with what dignity these two priests, one of whom has since been made a bishop, fulfilled their task, and how totally unpolitical they considered it to be. For them it was ecclesiastical and pastoral, and they were delighted with this new contact with the Catholic Church, whose representatives were in Rome from every continent. They were grateful that the Pope had not forgotten the millions of Orthodox Christians behind the Iron Curtain. The taking up of certain personal and diplomatic contacts with political representatives of the East had the same unpolitical, pastoral character. There was no question of intellectual capitulation to communism or of dismissing the witness of Christians who have suffered for their faith in many ways and continue to do so. On the contrary, it was a matter of helping these suffering Christians in their need, of alleviating their situation, of assisting the Church in these countries as much as possible, both its faithful and its pastors—with no reference to questions of prestige and of day-to-day politics.

The Pope's invitation to the Russian Orthodox observers and the consequent respect for their feelings prevented the Council from being misused for the purposes of a purely negative anti-communism, widespread in Southern Italy, which is strong in words and weak in deeds. One of the first official acts of the newly-elected pope was to improve the wages and the social standing of the Vatican employees. In practice and in theory he pursued social reforms. Was it surprising that this man, who felt for the poor of this country of vast class differences, with all his aversion for the communist system, should have little time for the anti-communism of those who fight communism with manifestoes and programmes alone, but who avoid social reforms wherever they can, support appalling corruption in the State administration, tolerate on the one hand unimaginable luxury, and on the other equally unimaginable misery, but who, when it comes to elections and other political

action, are always glad to enlist the aid of
the Church, its preaching and its pastoral
work, for their not particularly Christian
purposes?

In some circles Pope John has been blamed
for the increase in the communist vote at the
last Italian elections. Nothing is more unjust.
But if one wishes to defend Pope John against
this charge it will be necessary to bring out
into the open some facts which may possibly
shock. The responsibility for the increase in
the communist vote—apart from political
factors—rests largely with the failure of the
Italian Church to deal with the problems of
the moment. To put it bluntly, how long has
it, instead of preaching the gospel, preferred
to become involved in politics? Instead of
realising the gospel, preferred to distribute
pamphlets and collect votes? But how can a
Church be equipped for a positive confrontation with communism when its masses suffer
from appalling religious ignorance, from
superstition and poverty of belief (so often
the result of bad, moralizing or sentimental
sermons and superficial instruction which
bears little relation to life); when its clergy

—to the regret of many good Italian priests—
are educated within a seminary system as
insulated from the world as possible; when its
theology—to the regret of many gifted Italian
theologians—because of a fundamental lack
of intellectual freedom, has hardly produced
one work of international importance; when
its services—to the regret of many outstanding Catholic laymen—are unable to generate
any sense of Christian community; when it
has largely lost contact with the intellectuals
and with the workers? *This* is the problem of
communism in Italy, as far as it involves the
Church—in spite of all the fine and heroic
work that individual laymen and priests do,
often more than in our own countries. And it
was this that John XXIII sought to remedy:
by the universal renewal of the Church. He
could not fail to see that decrees of excom-
munication had achieved nothing in Italy,
but that the number of communist votes was
rising slowly but constantly even before his
pontificate. John XXIII wanted, with the
help of the Ecumenical Council, the positive
renewal of the Church and of religious
life especially within the Italian Church

and—precisely in order to combat anti-clericalism—a little more distance between the Church and internal Italian party politics. Didn't this involve taking certain risks? Better now than later! It was late enough, as it was. John XXIII, who saw further than his critics, wanted, through selfless service, to help remedy this situation.

OPEN TO ALL CHRISTIANS

John XXIII will go into church history as the pope who was able, as it were, overnight to bring the Church out of its reserve towards the ecumenical movement and make it ecumenically active. Of course there had been ecumenical endeavours before in the Catholic Church. But they involved only a tiny advanced guard of theologians and laymen. Pope John made the reunion of separated Christians a concern of the whole Church and particularly of its centre. Of course he was not the first to "open wide his arms"—as one used to say in Rome—towards other Christians. But it was generally an invitation to return, and nothing more. John XXIII was the first to show that opening one's arms was not enough, but that one also had to busy one's hands, in order to do one's own share of the work on the Catholic side to smooth the way towards reunion.

Preparation for reunion with separated Christians through the renewal of the Catholic Church itself! This was the tremendous programme he set the Second Vatican Council, this Council, which is essentially *his* Council. No-one forced him to do it, no-one advised him to do it. It was his decision and his programme. It was not as a great church strategist that he set in motion this epoch-making event. Church politics in the usual sense of the word were foreign to him. It was not even as a great theologian that he thought out this project full of dangers and of unforeseen possibilities, considered its dogmatic and historical basis, and worked out its theoretical and practical consequences. "Are you a theologian?" he asked a well-known Anglican minister. "No." "*Tant mieux*— neither am I!"

John XXIII conceived the idea of the Council out of the simple, childlike faith of a believing Christian convinced that with God's help something serious had to be done about the tragic divisions of the Church. He summoned this Council as a man of God who did not let himself be frightened by the risks of such an undertaking, but was always sustained by a holy optimism which was nothing other than unconquerable, realistic Christian hope. He knew the difficulties in the way of the idea of the Council in his immediate vicinity. But "Il concilio si deve fare malgrado la Curia"—"The Council must be held in spite of the Curia", he once said to some priests from his Bergamasque home, who were amazed that not everyone in Rome thought like the Pope.

He proceeded with caution and with great astuteness. He was helped by a quite unsentimental Christian love, which guided him in his everyday dealings. Hence his aversion for blind condemnations, thoughtless anathematisations and excommunications, against unjust inquisitional practices. He never offended anyone. He often achieved what he wanted inconspicuously and by apparently roundabout methods: "Papa Giovanni always gets what he's after", one of his friends told me. For a while he permitted his aides to pass over in silence the ecumenical purpose of the Council. "But I'll be bringing it in again," he said to a visitor who complained about it. And he founded the Secretariat for Promoting Christian Unity. An important factor in the success of the Council hitherto has been that the head of this Secretariat, Cardinal Bea, has always had, even in the most difficult undertakings, the Pope's full confidence.

John XXIII was a pragmatist who thought intuitively. And this was an advantage to the Council and to its ecumenical endeavours. This pope had no time for that doctrinalism which—because of its Pharisaism, its intolerance, and its lack of understanding for the genuine concerns of others—is the greatest and most dangerous enemy of the Council and of all ecumenical activity. That is why he told the theological preparatory commission not to prepare any formal new dogmas. Pope John was convinced that humanity is not best helped in its present situation by the repetition or definition of old truths, but by a proclamation of the Gospel appropriate to our own day, which will make use of new modes of expression and be able to distinguish between the substance and the trappings of the old teaching. He stated that with great emphasis to the Council in his opening address, and it has had great influence on the course of the Council's deliberations. John XXIII had no ambition to go down in history as a pope who, without being challenged by heresy, defined a new dogma. "I am not infallible", he once remarked in a conversation with Greek seminarians. When they looked at him in surprise, he said with a smile, "No, I'm not infallible. The Pope is infallible only when he speaks *ex cathedra*. But I will never speak *ex cathedra*." He never spoke *ex cathedra*.

In his ecumenical labours Pope John never bothered about questions of prestige, which largely prevent, or render purely formal the in themselves natural contacts and meetings between Christians (e.g., between Catholic and Lutheran bishops). The naturalness and warmth with which he received his non-Catholic visitors were often praised by them. During the Council he said to two brothers

from the Protestant community of Taizé, "Oh,
you've dressed in white!" "Normally we
dress in ordinary clothes," replied the
brothers, "but we put on this white robe for
services." "Oh, vous savez," laughed John, "je
ne suis pas jaloux!"—"I'm not jealous!" He
possessed great ecumenical tact and accepted
in natural friendliness, against all the reserva-
tions of protocol and of church diplomacy
which his advisers made, the gifts of Eastern
orthodox dignitaries and gave them presents
in return. A new sense of Christian brotherhood filled the heart of this bishop, who
always wanted to be a bishop among bishops
and who so often preferred not to bless the
people alone, but only with his brother
bishops. This new sense of Christian brotherhood prevented him from letting the Council
meet without the representatives of the other
Christian communities. When he received
them in the Vatican during the Council he
did not want to sit on the papal throne. He
asked for a chair and sat simply with them:
"For you I am not Peter's successor!"

Let no one say that these things are trifles.
They reveal a whole attitude. They succeeded

in changing the whole climate. During the five years of his pontificate the ecumenical situation improved more than in fifty years, indeed, almost more than in five hundred years. Is it surprising that all men of good will—to whom he dedicated his last encyclical, *Pacem in terris*—are grateful to him, and that not only Christians, but also Jews, whom he was particularly fond of, prayed for his life? All these men realised that here was a man who only wanted to serve: the Church, Christendom, the world, all men. Right up to his painful death, about which he had known for a long time, he endured in this service without drawing any attention to himself whatsoever.

The Catholic Church, after John XXIII, can never be the same again. A new era of church history started with him, an era of new life, of new freedom, of new hope. His last wish on his death-bed was that the Council might continue and bring forth abundantly. Of course there will be fresh opposition and fresh difficulties in the way of his programme. But the Catholic Church will continue along the road that John XXIII has opened up. His programme—the renewal of the Church and reunion with separated Christians—has not only a pope, but the Lord of the Church himself behind it.

DEEPENING OF THE NEW SENSE OF THE CHURCH

U NLIKE the first session of Vatican II, the second opened in an atmosphere of hope and initiative. Pope Paul VI's improvement of the conciliar machinery and his address on the reform of the Roman Curia had been very welcome to the episcopate and the Church. The programme outlined in the Pope's great speech at the opening of the second session was equally remarkable for its courage and its clarity. The Council, said Pope Paul, was to continue with energy and decision along the course set by John XXIII. The Council itself is seen in theological depth as a representation of the Church:

Indeed, this solemn assembly of brothers, to which eminent men have come together from East and West, from North and South, well deserves the noble and prophetic name of Church: that is, of community, of those called together. Indeed, here is fulfilled anew that saying which comes to our mind at the sight of this assembly: "Their sound hath gone forth into all the earth, and their words unto the ends of the whole world." [Rom. 10.18; Ps. 18.5.] May all those hidden characteristics of the Church shine forth, because of which we designate her as the one and Catholic Church! By this assembly, in which the whole Church is made visible, we are led to consider not only her apostolic origin, which is as it were portrayed before our eyes in this ceremony, but also her goal, the effective sanctification of men, for which the Church beloved by us is striving. Here the marks that characterize the Church are made visible.[1]

With a clarity unparalleled in any Pope since the Reformation, Pope Paul threw into sharp relief the figure of *Christ as the origin, the way and the goal* of the Council and the Church:

[1] From the text of the speech given in *Herder-Korrespondenz*, 18 (1963–4), pp. 76–83. Cf. pt. 2, ch. 1, of Hans Küng, *The Living Church*, London, Sheed and Ward (1963).

The answer is Christ: Christ from whom we begin; Christ who is both the road we travel and our guide on the way; Christ, our hope and our final end.

O, may this Council be fully aware of this relationship between ourselves and Jesus Christ, a relationship which has a hundred different aspects yet is always the same, which stands firm yet is the source of life and movement, full of mystery yet limpid in its clarity, a relationship which demands much from us, yet fills us with joy. May the Council be deeply conscious of this relationship between the holy and living Church—which is really our own selves —and Christ, from whom we come, by whom we live, and towards whom we go.

Let there be no other guiding light for this gathering but Christ, the light of the world. Let the interest of our minds be turned to no other truth but the words of the Lord, our one master . . . [1]

[1] *Council Speeches of Vatican II*, ed. Yves Congar, O.P., Hans Küng and Daniel O'Hanlon, S.J., London, Sheed and Ward (1964), p. 11.

Starting from this Christocentric point of departure, the Council is set the following four principal tasks: (1) A deepening of the Church's understanding of herself; (2) Renewal of the Church; (3) The restoration of unity between all Christians; (4) Dialogue between the Church and the men of our time.

The opening speech provided a number of points from which to develop a deepening of the Church's understanding of herself:

(a) Strong emphasis was laid on the character of the Papacy as service: "The least amongst you, the servant of the servants of God", desires "to show you in a concrete way that he wants to be with you, to pray with you, talk with you, reflect and work with you".

Here at the beginning of the second session of this great Synod, we testify before God that we advance no claims of any kind to worldly power and cherish no desire of any kind for personal dominion, but have only one wish and will: to carry out that divine commission by which we have been called, brethren, by you all, to be the chief shepherd amongst you.

He, Pope Paul VI, "new in the papal service", wanted to see himself as like his predecessor, Honorius III, in the great mosaic of Christ in St. Paul's Outside the Walls:

> The small figure of the Pope is repre-
> sented there prostrate, kissing the feet of a
> Christ of gigantic dimensions. This Christ,
> in the likeness of a royal and majestic
> teacher, presides over and blesses the
> people gathered in the basilica—a symbol
> of the Church.[1]

(b) The episcopate is seen as a brotherly communion, a college: "You yourselves go back to the college of the Apostles, whose true heirs you are. Here we are united in prayer by the same faith and the same love." The Pope was looking forward to the discussion about the status of the bishops "confidently and expectantly":

> Taking for granted the dogmatic declara-
> tions of Vatican I concerning the Roman
> Pontiff, we confidently and expectantly

[1] *Council Speeches*, p. 12. Cf. *The Living Church*, pt. 5, ch. 2.

look forward to this discussion which shall develop the doctrine of the episcopate, its function and its relationship with Peter.

For us personally, it will provide doctrinal and practical standards by which our apostolic office, endowed though it is by Christ with the fullness and sufficiency of power, may receive more help and support . . .[1]

(c) The whole Church is seen "as a community established in this world, visible and hierarchically ordered, but at the same time animated from within by a mysterious force"; not only as the Mystical Body but at the same time as "the building raised up by Christ, the house of God, the temple and tabernacle of God, his people, his flock, his vine, his field, his city. . . ."[2] The Church is seen not only in her unity with Christ but also in her distinctness from him: she is "on pilgrimage", "a pilgrimage through this world and time", "a pilgrim Church". "Deformations in her face

[1] *Council Speeches*, pp. 16–17. Cf. *The Living Church*, pt. 5, ch. 1.
[2] *Council Speeches*, p. 15.

2

or in her bridal garment" are not passed over in silence. The Church is called upon to show "the most loyal obedience to the words and teachings of Christ", "submission to the light of the Holy Spirit, who is clearly at this time demanding of the Church that she should do everything to appear before men as that which she is".[1]

(d) The Church's service of the world is given impressive prominence: the Church's approach to the world is one of "sincere admiration and the sincere intention, not of dominating it, but of serving it; not of despising it, but of appreciating it; not of condemning it, but of strengthening and saving it".[2] Special attention is paid to the poor, the needy, the sorrowful; to the workers; to the representatives of intellectual life and the sciences (it is the Church's wish to "defend their liberty"), to political rulers. Especially positive things are said not only to the young, advancing nations but also to the great world religions, "which preserve the sense and

[1] Cf. *The Living Church*, pt. 5, ch. 1.
[2] *Council Speeches*, p. 155.

notion of the one supreme transcendent God, creator and sustainer, and which worship him with acts of sincere piety".[1]

In these religions the Catholic Church sees, not without regret, omissions, insufficiencies and errors. But equally, she cannot help addressing herself to them to say that the Catholic religion recognizes, with due reverence, all that is true and good and human in them, and at the same time to affirm that she will be first and foremost when it comes to protecting, in the men of our day, the sense of religion and reverence for God, which are the foundation of the common good, and effectively defending, as it were, God's rights over men.[2]

The second version of the *schema* on the Church, *De Ecclesia*, was indeed a notable improvement on the first, though it was still in many respects unsatisfying. The month-long debate (30 September to 31 October 1963) emphasized a whole series of points of

[1] *Council Speeches*, p. 156.
[2] Cf. *The Living Church*, pt. 5, ch. 2.

view of crucial importance for the image of the Church in our day; points which indicate a turning away from the juridical, triumphalist, clericalist idea of the Church belonging to the Counter-Reformation, and a growing trend towards the scriptural idea of the Church. These points of view can be seen in all their impressive concreteness in some of the conciliar speeches now published[1]: they can only be schematically summarized here:

(1) The Church as the eschatological People of God of the New Covenant, to which all, laity and those who bear office, belong;

(2) The preaching of the word of God and the celebration of baptism and the Eucharist as constitutive of the Church, which thus exists essentially as the local Church, the community;

(3) The sinfulness of the Church in this world, and hence her constant dependence upon God's forgiveness;

(4) The charismatic, pneumatic structure of the Church in the New Testament, built not only on the Apostles but on the Prophets, in which the Holy Spirit is given to *all* Chris-

[1] See *Council Speeches*.

tians, and each individual Christian has his particular spiritual gift, his special charism for the building up of the community;

(5) The sharing of each individual Christian in the universal priesthood of the faithful, who form, all together, a royal prophetical and priestly people and are all, without exception, called to evangelical perfection and holiness;

(6) The function of office in the Church as selfless, brotherly service towards the individual Christian and the whole great People of God, in which *all* are brothers under one Lord;

(7) The special importance of prophets and teachers (theologians) alongside the Apostles and their successors;

(8) The brotherly association of the bishops, who form a college having, together with the Pope, a common, corporate responsibility for the whole Church;

(9) The theological significance of sacramental episcopal consecration, by which an individual is accepted into the college of bishops and receives his authority from Christ;

(10) The rightfulness of the priesthood, and the association of bishops and priests together in one single service of the Church;

(11) The restoration of the permanent diaconate, on the model of the early Church;

(12) The necessity of multiplicity and freedom within the one Church and the meaning of different traditions, especially those of both West *and* East, as manifesting the Church's catholicity;

(13) The missionary structure not only of the "missionary Churches" but of the Church as a whole, and the special relation of the Church to the poor;

(14) The Church's service of the world and care for men of other religions and races;

(15) The positive aspect of a separation of Church and State.

One of the two questions which caused most excitement in the Council was the common, collegiate responsibility of the bishops, together with the Pope, for the whole Church. A balanced adjustment of the definition of the primacy made at Vatican I is urgently called for both by Scripture and by the present situation of the Church, but powerful curial forces ranged themselves against this, even trying to bypass the second text of the *schema*. Speeches for and against the collegiality of the episcopate were almost evenly balanced in the debate. But when it came to the historic "test vote" of 30 October 1963 (which has been called the Catholic Church's "October Revolution"), the following question was given an affirmative answer by 1808 votes to 336: "Is it the wish of the Fathers that the *schema* be so worded as to state that the body or college of bishops is, in its preaching, sanctifying and pastoral office, the successor of the Apostolic College, and that it is endowed, together with its head, the Roman Pope, and never without that head (whose primacy in respect of all the pastors and faithful remains undisputed and undiminished), with full and supreme authority over the whole Church?"

The other question that aroused vigorous controversy (because of its connection with celibacy), the introduction of a permanent diaconate, was also given an affirmative answer at this provisional vote, by 1588 to

525. The question of married deacons was wisely left open.

A book could be written on each of the fifteen themes listed above. Books have in fact been written about each of them. The whole debate on the Church showed that the work done during the last few decades by exegetes, historians and dogmatic theologians in the "advance guard" of the Church—work that has often been misjudged and brought under suspicion—has not been in vain but is at last bearing fruit a hundredfold. Certainly, along with the voices that expressed "open" views there were many voices to be heard simply defending the *status quo*; but they were not representative of the great majority of the Council. Certainly much that was said in this discussion will, even in ten years' time, seem like a very modest beginning. Certainly there is a great deal being said in scholarly Catholic theology today that was not stated in the debate. But if no more than half of all the positive and constructive things said in the *aula* by the bishops is made by the Theological Commission to bear fruit in the new *schema* on the Church, Catholic ecclesiology will still have taken a mighty step forward. This, at any rate, is something that the Second Vatican Council has made clear: in ecclesiology, too, the period of the Counter-Reformation is past, once and for all.

3

WIDENING OF THE ECUMENICAL OPENING

JOHN XXIII, a charismatic servant-Pope, brought about the ecumenical opening more by deeds—often small but very eloquent deeds—than by words. His deeply ecumenical approach, not primarily a product of academic reflection, swept the Church along with it; a Church which had been prepared for this for decades by theological and practical work. But the ecumenical breakthrough in the whole Church, brought about by the first session, is urgently in need of deepening, including intellectual and theological deepening. Here, too, Paul VI's opening speech gave the Council a supremely important lead on many points[1]:

(a) Outside the Church, according to the Pope, there are not only individual Christians, but "Christian communions worthy of

[1] Cf. *The Living Church*, pt. 1, ch. 2.

reverence". This recognition, long passed over in official circles, is important to the very foundations of ecumenical work.

(b) The ecumenical dialogue requires absolute honesty and the renunciation of confessional polemic:

> Our manner of speaking towards them is friendly, completely sincere and loyal. We lay no snares. We are not motivated by temporal interests. We owe our Faith—which we believe to be divine—the most candid and firm attachment.

> But at the same time we are convinced that this does not constitute an obstacle to the desired understanding with our separated brethren, precisely because it is the truth of the Lord and therefore the principle of union, not of distinction or separation. At any rate, we do not wish to make of our Faith an occasion for polemics.[1]

(c) The "utmost possible multiplicity in unity" is explicitly approved:

> For recent movements, at present in full development in bodies of Christians sepa-

[1] *Council Speeches*, pp. 96–7.

rated from us, show clearly two things. The
first is that the Church of Christ is one
alone and therefore must be unique. The
second is that this mystic and visible union
cannot be attained except in identity of
faith, and by participation in the same
sacraments and in the organic harmony of
a single ecclesiastical direction, even though
this allows for a great variety of verbal
expressions, movements, lawful institutions
and preference with regard to modes of
acting.[1]

(d) Not only do the other Christian communions share a common religious inherit-
ance with us, but they have themselves
developed this heritage in a positive way; this,
as all know, is the first time that a Pope has
clearly stated this:

> We look with reverence upon the true
> religious patrimony we share in common,
> which has been preserved and in part even
> well developed among our separated
> brethren.[2]

[1] *Council Speeches*, p. 95.
[2] *Council Speeches*, p. 97.

The efforts of ecumenically minded theologians on both sides, striving to see the truth in the opposite side, are explicitly praised:

> We are pleased to note the study made by those who seek sincerely to make known and to honour the treasures of truth and of genuine spirituality, in order to improve our relations with them.
>
> We hope that just as they are desirous to know more about our history and our religious life, that they would also wish to make a closer study of our doctrine and its logical derivation from the deposit of divine revelation.[1]

(e) A truly historic act, which aroused the attention of Christians of all communions, was the confession of guilt which the Pope made, with visible emotion; the first Pope to do so since Adrian VI in Luther's day. In the spirit of the Gospel, he asked for, and gave, forgiveness:

> If we are in any way to blame for that separation, we humbly beg God's forgive-

[1] *Council Speeches*, p. 97.

ness. And we ask pardon, too, of our
brethren who feel themselves to have been
injured by us. For our part, we willingly
forgive the injuries which the Catholic
Church has suffered, and forget the grief
endured during the long series of dissen-
sions and separations. May the heavenly
Father deign to hear our prayers and grant
us true brotherly peace.[1]

The Pope expressed the same thought even
more forcibly in his address on 17 October
1963 to the observers from the other Christian Churches:

In our speech of 29 September 1963, we
made bold to appeal for Christian forgiveness—so far as possible, on both sides.
"Veniam demus petimusque vicissim."
[Horace.] We need this peace, if we wish to
attain to friendly relations and honest discussion. And above all, because it is Christian, as our Lord says: "If therefore thou
offer thy gift at the altar, and there thou
remember that thy brother hath anything

[1] *Council Speeches*, p. 96.

against thee; leave there thy offering before the altar, and go first to be reconciled to thy brother; and then coming thou shalt offer thy gift." [Matt. 5.23–4.]

The fact that the reunion of separated Christians—ecumenism, to give it its inelegant and easily misunderstood Latin name—was discussed at the Second Vatican Council at all was in itself an event in Church history of incalculable consequence. Here too there were, of course, contrary voices. But they were even more isolated and less representative than in other debates. The *schema De Oecumenismo*, incorporating and combining the ecumenical texts presented to the first session by the Theological Commission and the Commission for the Eastern Churches, had been prepared by the Secretariat for Christian Unity under the leadership of Cardinal Bea, and was of an exceptionally high standard. This immediately had a good effect on the debate, in that there was less need for negative criticism and the discussion could be concentrated more on positive and constructive points. It was a great experience to find impressive voices being raised for "ecumenism" (which is not meant as a theory and doctrine but as a pastoral movement and activity), not only from Central Europe but also from Italy, Spain, North and South America, Africa and Asia. The discussion lasted from 18 November till the end of the session, and has not yet been wound up.

The *schema* itself is not intended to deal comprehensively and exhaustively with everything that there is to be said on the subject of preparing for the reunion of separated Christians. It aims rather at assembling a number of pastoral principles and pointers required by the present situation so as to give an effective lead, in the various sectors of the field, to serious preparation for reunion from the Catholic side. Thus it is primarily intended for Catholics themselves, according to the sound ecumenical principle that each Church should begin *with itself*, and above all should seriously *make a beginning*, all along the line. In a few years' time more theological and practical experience will have accumulated, and it will be possible to say still more.

Even in the *schema* as it stands, it is
admitted that the other communions have
their part to play in the divine plan of re-
demption, and what there is in common between the Catholic Church and the other
Christian Churches is strongly emphasized
and taken as a basis for a further drawing
together and a greater degree of common life.
We are called upon to avoid everything that
could hinder reunion and do everything that
will assist it. The reform of the Catholic
Church—liturgical, biblical and pastoral
renewal—is strongly emphasized as the necessary condition for reunion, and so is the
necessity for interior conversion and a truly
evangelical life in the individual Catholic.
There follow some practical directives on
common prayer by Catholics and other Christians, on improvement of each side's knowledge of the other and on the ecumenical
dialogue, on ecumenical training for clergy
and laity, theological students and mission-
aries, on an ecumenical presentation of the
Catholic faith, and on practical co-operation
with other Christians.

Here, again, the discussion produced valu-

able additions and amendments; the Secretariat for Unity had announced in advance
that all improvements would be extremely
welcome. For many non-Catholic Christians,
certainly, the *schema* as presented would be
in many ways dissatisfying; too juridical and
too static. They find it hard to understand,
for instance, how the Catholic Church can
maintain that all other Churches have only
parts of the truth while she has the totality of
truth, considering that the Catholic Church,
too, has for long periods forgotten, overlooked
and neglected many truths of the Gospel. To
apply the word "Churches" only to the Orthodox, not the Protestant Churches, involves an
unnecessary repulse to many Protestants. The
criterion of episcopal government (or, bound
up with this, of the Eucharist) seems arbitrary,
and not to do justice to the problems of the
Protestant Reformation. In the case of many
Communions with an episcopal Church
order, such as the Anglican Church or the
Swedish Lutherans, it would be difficult to
say whether they should be called a "Church"
or only a "community", *communitas* (the invalidity of Anglican Orders remains, even

since the ruling of Leo XIII neither definitive nor infallible), a matter of historical controversy, and the invalidity of the Eucharist celebrated outside the Catholic Church and the Orthodox Churches is not so easily demonstrated theologically as it often appears). We cannot simply introduce at will any number of elements and conditions into our definition of "Church", or we shall succumb to an unscriptural narrowing of the concept (as did Bellarmine, for instance, by incorporating submission to the primacy into the definition of "Church", so that he was consequently unable to recognize even the Orthodox Churches as "Churches"). It would be theologically sound and ecumenically fruitful to take as our framework and starting-point some minimal concept, such as: The name "Church" can be applied to any community, universally ordered and grounded on Holy Scripture, of baptized Christians, who believe in Christ the Lord, intend to celebrate the Eucharist, seek to live according to the Gospel, and wish to be called a Church. To bring into prominence this foundation of common ecclesial ground would constitute, in itself, an urgent summons to deepen the common life and the ecclesial character of the community.

In the course of the debate, then, the demand was made in due form that the Protestant Churches too should be called Churches. At the same time a confession of the Catholic share of guilt for the division of the Churches was called for, and a critical confrontation with the truth, for which room and freedom had not always been sufficiently allowed in the Catholic Church. The positive meaning of the division of the Churches in the history of salvation should be brought out: God's gracious providence should be recognized even in human divisions. Conversion, meaning conversion to Christ, should be demanded of everyone, Catholics included. In particular, intellectual humility was needed in regard to the other Christian communions. Freedom for theologians in their work was a necessity for the ecumenical encounter[1] etc. We may expect important improvements to the *schema*, since there is no doubt that the various suggestions made to

[1] Cf. *Council Speeches*.

the Secretariat for Unity are being turned to good account.

There is also good reason to hope that proposals made in the debate about practical problems will receive serious attention. This applies, for instance, to revision of outdated juristic regulations about participation by Catholics in the religious services of other Christians and vice versa (*communicatio in sacris*), a question of particular importance to the Eastern Churches. But it applies above all to the problem of mixed marriages the urgency of which is still not always sufficiently realized in Catholic areas, whereas for the man in the street in our countries it is apt to head the list of conciliar expectations. Millions of Christians suffer, directly or indirectly, from this problem; millions have been unnecessarily alienated from the Catholic Church because of it. Are facts like this really being adequately faced? A parish priest in an ordinary parish where Catholics are in a minority recently told me, with great distress, that of all the marriages in the parish 59% are mixed marriages and 41% *invalid* mixed marriages (with, in addition, 6% invalid in

which both partners are Catholics). With
almost half the marriages in a parish ecclesiastically invalid, the children illegitimate
in the eyes of Church law, how is it possible
to do any reasonable kind of pastoral work?
It is easy to understand that the courageous
proposal of the Cardinal of Cologne to recognize marriages performed outside the Church
as valid has been hailed with joy and hope
in Germany, by Catholic and Protestants,
clergy and laity alike. There is, besides, a
widespread expectation that later on the question of the upbringing of the children of a
mixed marriage will call for an adjustment
making possible a theologically admissible
solution of the problem of a genuine clash of
consciences.

As early as 21 November a vote was taken
on accepting as a basis for discussion the first
three chapters of the ecumenical *schema*
(guiding principles of the ecumenical movement, practice in the ecumenical movement,
our attitude towards Christians separated
from the Catholic Church). This was agreed
by over 95%. This vote shows what a vast
distance we have come in the last five years.

A similar vote on Chapters 4 and 5 was envisaged as to take place "soon", but, to the great disappointment of many both within the Council and outside, it never happened. Both Chapter 4, on the relation of Christians to Jews, and Chapter 5, on religious freedom, were eventually printed, after many difficulties had arisen, and distributed to the Fathers. World attention was caught when it became known that the Catholic Church, after long centuries of overt or covert anti-Semitism within her bounds, but for which the Nazi hatred of the Jews would not have been thinkable, was proposing to correct certain deeply-rooted religious prejudices against the ancient People of God, though without involving itself in any political question (the State of Israel). The presentation of Chapter 4 by the German curial Cardinal Bea, who spoke with great frankness about the Nazi persecution of the Jews, was received in the Council with as much applause as the introduction of the chapter on religious freedom by Bishop De Smedt of Bruges. Since the question of religious freedom is one of basic importance in a modern, pluralist society and regarded as a top priority by, for instance, the episcopate of the United States, it is particularly regrettable that time could not be found for the proposed vote on the general suitability of these two chapters for discussion. But Cardinal Bea solemnly promised that postponement would not mean that these questions had been shelved, and that both chapters would be dealt with at the next session. Now that these questions have been formally proposed, they must be given an answer, and an affirmative one. Even the mere fact of the presentation of these two chapters constitutes an ecumenical event of the first importance.

When we survey everything done, or at least set promisingly in motion, during this second session, in the ecumenical sector, the question imposes itself whether it will be fully appreciated on the Orthodox and Protestant side. There ought to be sincere rejoicing over these workings of the Spirit and this simply fantastic ecumenical development in the Catholic Church during the last three or four years; not (as one does still encounter here and there) an unnecessary worsening of the difficulties of our forward advance by taking up an aloof attitude, through fear, acknowledged or unacknowledged, for one's own position, or being unconstructively hypercritical of what has been achieved and aggressively calculating about what is "still not forthcoming". Constructive criticism, which is at the same time self-critical, is always welcome. But the crucial point is this: Is there going to be a pharisaically unrepentant totting-up of how many steps the Catholic Church is now "at last" taking in the wake of the Reformation, or are people going to embark in their own Churches on renewal and reform and ecumenical understanding with the same determination as has been shown so far in the Second Vatican Council? Karl Barth, with his unerring sense for the essential, is the man who has grasped more than any other in the Protestant world the greatness of the challenge being presented to the Churches of the Reformation by the Catholic Church now filled with a new evangelical spirit.[1] Not only the rank and file

[1] K. Barth, "Thoughts on the Second Vatican Council", in *The Ecumenical Review*, 15 (1963), pp. 357–66. Cf. K. G. Steck, who has written as follows

in the Protestant Churches but also the theologians and Church leaders, not only in
America but in Europe too, are becoming
more and more aware of the urgent need for
a positive Protestant response to the event of

---

of the reform set on foot in the Catholic Church by
the Council: "It is not only a movement concerned
with better adaptation to the present day but a movement springing from the Gospel and directed towards
the Gospel. But what can this mean for modern Reformation Protestantism? What happens when, in the
expression used in a lay discussion, the barriers get
too low? When we have to recognize and say that the
Gospel has grown and is growing in strength in the
Roman World? The Reformation never denied that
Roman Christendom, like all Christendom, drew its
life from the Gospel. But it did not recognize in the
Roman Church the true Church nor, in the voice of
the Pope, the voice of the one Good Shepherd. What
is going to happen if the lines drawn in the sixteenth
century really become pointless? That they have not
become so yet, by any means, has been seen and said
clearly enough in connection with the Council itself.
But we are already faced with the question of what
Reformation Protestantism really is today. If it is only
a more or less successful imitation of Romanism – and
there are times when it understands and presents itself in this way – then it will become more superflous
than ever, whatever barriers it may erect round itself.
Is it perhaps on the contrary the critical complement

the Council and an effective ecumenical advance towards the Catholic Church. This is a ground for rejoicing and hope.

---

of the Catholic expression of our common Christian heritage? In that case it might perhaps be content with the possession of a certain number of niches and altars within the Roman pantheon. Or is it the true Church in the original, New-Testament sense, set, as ever, over against the Roman Church as the Church of Anti-christ? But who can make such statements without faltering?

If we are not mistaken, the Council, whatever its further development may be, has confronted modern Reformation Protestantism with the basic question of its own task and nature more sharply than at any time, at least since the sixteenth century, and perhaps – the Roman phenomenon over against us having changed as it has – more sharply than ever before. [Quoted from Herder–Korrespondenz, 18 (1963–4), pp. 100f.]

4

WE KNOW IN PART

I T was striking that in that part of his opening address which Pope Paul devoted to
John XXIII he emphasized nothing so
strongly as his predecessor's rejection of that
doctrinalism which, disregarding pastoral
and ecumenical perspectives, delights in a
sterile verbal repetition of "tradition" and an
unselfcritical condemnation of all who think
otherwise.[1] Like John XXIII, Paul VI is convinced that the pastoral orientation of the
Council "appears more urgent and fruitful
now than ever". The Pope spoke thus in
praise of his predecessor:

> . . . you declared: "Nor is the primary pur-
> pose of our work to discuss one article or
> another of the fundamental doctrine of the
> Church", but rather, "to consider how to
> expound Church teaching in a manner

[1] Cf. *The Living Church*, pt. 1, ch. 1; pt. 2, ch. 2;
pt. 4, ch. 2.

demanded by the times". [*AAS* (1962), pp. 791–2.]

You have strengthened the convictions of the teaching authority of the Church regarding Christian doctrine. It is not only truth to be investigated by reason illumined by faith, but it is also the generative word of life and action. You have strengthened our opinion that the authority of the Church ought not to be limited to the condemnation of errors. Rather, this authority should be extended to proclaim that positive and vital doctrine which is the source of its fecundity.

The teaching office of the Church, which is neither wholly theoretical nor wholly negative, must in the Council manifest ever more the lifegiving power of the message of Christ, who said: "The words that I have spoken to you are spirit and life." [John 6.64.][1]

The Council is explicitly called upon to continue in the pastoral and ecumenical

[1] *Council Speeches*, p. 10. Cf. *The Living Church*, pt. 4, ch. 2.

direction so powerfully initiated by John XXIII:

Hence we shall ever keep in mind thy norms which you, the first Father of this Council, have wisely laid down and which we may profitably repeat here: "Our task is not merely to guard this precious treasure, namely our Faith, as if we were only concerned with antiquity, but to dedicate ourselves with an earnest will and without fear to that work which our era demands of us, pursuing thus the path which the Church has followed for nearly twenty centuries. Hence, that method of presenting the truth must be used which is more in conformity with a *magisterium* prevalently pastoral in character." [*AAS* (1962), pp. 791–2.]

We shall have due regard for the great question of the unity in one flock of those who believe in Christ and wish to be members of the Church which you, John, have called the paternal home whose doors are open to all. The Council which you have promoted and inaugurated will proceed faithfully along the path you pointed out, so that with God's help may it reach the goal you have so ardently desired and hoped for.[1]

Hence it is no wonder that the Pope also explicitly stated his wish that in the doctrine *De Ecclesia* itself preference should be given to pastoral and ecumenical explanations over solemn definitions:

It moreover seems to us that the time has now come to more and more examine, co-ordinate and explore the truth about the Church of Christ. Perhaps the expression should not take the form of a solemn dogmatic definition. Rather the Church should declare by a more serious and clear magisterium what she considers herself to be.[2]

The Council, which had already, in the first session, sharply rejected traditionalist, apologetic and polemical doctrinalism, gave an attentive and delighted reception to these parts of the Pope's speech. And both the de-

[1] *Council Speeches*, p. 10. Cf. *The Living Church*, pt. 4, ch. 2.

[2] *Council Speeches*, p. 16. Cf. *The Living Church*, pt. 1, ch. 1; pt. 4, ch. 2; pt. 4, ch. 3.

bates on the Church and those on the reunion of separated Christians showed that the intention is to go firmly on along the course that has been begun. While these debates have given expression to a mass of positive starting-points for the pastoral and ecumenical statement of Catholic doctrine, it has also become clear that theological reflection is not a simple matter, that it calls for extremely thorough exegetical, historical and systematic research, and that even in a few years' time it will be possible to say a great deal much better, on a much deeper foundation, and in a much more balanced way, than it is now.

Hence it is not only the pastoral and ecumenical but also the specifically theological point of view that calls for the greatest restraint and moderation in doctrinal statements. We are more than ever aware today of the contingent character of conciliar decrees, on account of numerous exegetical and historical studies, and of the theological experience of the last few decades.

It has always been known in the Church that not even conciliar decrees fall from heaven; that even decisions of the Church ecumenically assembled in the Holy Spirit are the work of men and the words of men. And hence it is today common ground amongst Catholic theologians that conciliar decrees have to be historically interpreted: What did the Fathers of the Council mean by their words, in that place and time—what did they really mean? What was the situation, as regards the history of thought and the history of theology, in which they spoke? What state of affairs and what opponents had they in view? What theological schools and personalities were behind their opinion? What non-theological factors affected their judgement? At what points did they intend, or not intend, to speak with binding force?

A great deal can be built up from precise historical analysis of the texts of the decrees and from thorough study of the acts of a Council, if available. But there is a great difference between studying a conciliar decree in Denzinger's *Enchiridion Symbolorum, Definitionum et Declarationum*, or even in Mansi's many volumes of the acts of the Councils, *Sacrorum Conciliorum Nova et Amplissima Collectio*, and simply being

3

present at an Ecumenical Council. It is a fascinating experience for a theologian to follow the genesis of a conciliar decree, "live", from inside.

At a Council, one experiences the contingent character of conciliar decrees in a concrete way that makes it quite different from studying the acts of the Councils. It is only to a certain, often quite minimal, degree that the things that determine the wording of a decree find their way into the acts. But if you are actually there, you have concrete experience of what all the thousand and one "chances" of the Council's day-to-day life have meant to a decree and the detailed formulae used in it. Not only that *this* commission, with *this* president and secretary, prepared the decree; that it had precisely the introduction that it did have to the *plenum*, and not some other; that this was followed by *these* interventions rather than others; that *these* rather than *those* members of the commission revised it, and so on. But also that during that particular hour it was not the president but the vice-president who was in the chair; that at one of the innumerable *ricevimenti* that particular Protestant observer had a chance to draw the attention of this particular bishop to such-and-such a problem; that this term rather than that was used in the third question put by the moderators in the test vote; that at this or that meeting this or that member happened to be there or not there; that some particular bishop or *peritus* was able to make his point because his Latin was good, or had to keep quiet because it was not; that such-and-such a commission or secretariat contained scarcely a single exegete abreast of the current situation in his field; that some bishops' conference did or did not summon up its energies to make a contribution to the debate; that a particular private co-ordinating group of bishops and theologians were right in their estimate of how a debate or a vote would go; that such-and-such a bishop had one particular theologian at his disposal for working out his speeches, or that such-and-such a theologian found a bishop who was prepared to bring up the point he was concerned with in the *aula*.

It is often almost terrifying to realize how, in the turmoil of Vatican II, with its nearly three thousand participants, it may depend on a single man whether some particular important matter gets stated in the Council or not, and consequently whether or not it finds its way into the decree. Later on, it will be practically impossible to establish why it was that this or that point of view, important to the ecumenical dialogue, did get into the *schema* on the Church while some other one did not, because it will no longer be possible to realize what things did or did not take place, outside protocol, in the way of more or less chance ideas, forgetfulnesses, observations, encounters, contacts and meetings.

Now, there is nothing bad about the fact that all this will no longer be known; details as such are not so important as all that. But what would be bad would be if it were later to be forgotten how human the work of a Council composed of human beings is, even in those of its decrees which are meant to stand for centuries; if eternal value comes to be ascribed to what is in fact temporally conditioned; if people expect to find *everything* where everything is simply not to be found. How often it has happened that later commentators have tried to pin a Council down over something on which the Council itself did not commit itself at all!

It is true—and Protestant theology would do well to give more serious consideration to this question—that the words of a Council, which seeks to give expression to the unanimous faith of the whole Church, possess a binding character altogether different from that of the view of an individual theologian who speaks only for himself. And the whole Church is able to speak "in the Holy Spirit" in a quite different sense from the individual theologian, who is in a quite different way at the mercy of his own "spirit". If the special binding character of conciliar statements of doctrine is overlooked, then that "doctrinal chaos" so often deplored in the Protestant world is the inevitable result.

But, while giving all due emphasis to the binding character of the Church's formulations of her belief, Catholic theology and individual conciliar interpreters should never forget, particularly after Vatican II, what we may, following St Paul, call the *fragmentary* character of the Church's statements of doctrine: "We know in part, and we prophesy in part. But when that which is perfect is come, that which is in part shall be done away . . . We see now through a glass in a dark manner: but then face to face." (1 Cor. 13.9–12.) If the imperfect, incomplete, enigmatic, partial, fragmentary character of all our formulations of our faith is really taken seriously in connection with Vatican II, then there is no danger that its decrees will, by reason of deficiencies which it is only to be expected they will contain, hinder and restrict the ecumenical dialogue instead of advancing it. The fact that, as far as can be seen, both Council and Pope mean to refrain from new infallible dogmas in favour of "declarations" shows that there is more awareness at Vatican II than there was at Vatican I of this fragmentary character. In this way there will be no barring of any road that offers hope; rather, all doors will be left open to new knowledge and progress. Who knows? Perhaps the time may even come when awareness that the word "infallibility" expresses the binding but not the fragmentary character of the Church's formulations of her faith will lead to the discovery of a comprehensive, balanced concept that includes both, with the true and permanent content of each.

In this connection, a brief note on one question of special delicacy which was passionately discussed at the Council: On 29 October, by a bare majority of forty, the Council decided in favour of integrating the *schema* on Mary into that on the Church, and against the separate *schema* (which the Theological Commission had presented for discussion again, after a year, with a new title but otherwise unaltered!). Amongst the minority, where the predominant grounds were those of feeling, the opinion was widely held that only a separate *schema* on Mary as "Mother of the Church" (a title which has no foundation in Catholic tradition) would give her the honour that is her due. It may be remarked, merely in passing, that what would then first be called for would be a *schema* on "Christ the Lord of the Church", in harmony with the Pope's opening speech; it was certainly no accident that he spoke of "Christ the one Mediator between God and man". To the majority, whose spokesman was Cardinal Koenig, it seemed that a sound theological treatment of Mary's position could only be given within the Church, within the great community of believers of the New-Testament People of God, of which the first and pre-eminent member is she whose glory it is that she believed: "Blessed art thou that hast believed!" (Luke 1.45.) The dangers of Mariolatry, or at least of unhealthy excesses in isolated, emotional, unscriptural Mariology and Marian devotion, obscuring the one Mediator, Jesus Christ, were pointed out to the Council by, amongst others, the South American bishops. A Mariology that is more scriptural, ecumenical, soundly pastoral and integrated into ecclesiology is happily becoming more and more established in the Church. With this narrow result in the voting it is, of course, going to be very difficult to work out a *schema* on this question that will please both sides. But it would be better to have no Marian *schema* at all than one that does not help us, theologically, ecumenically and pastorally, in directing the whole People of God, in union with Mary, towards Christ: "Whatsoever he shall say to you, do ye." (John 2.5.)[1]

[1] One of the very few bishops who was already drawing attention to aberrations in Marian devotion

It is easily seen that one thing that is of crucial importance in all the questions of the Church's renewal and the reunion of separated Christians is a *theology* which goes back afresh to its origins, which thinks scripturally, historically and concretely. It was not in vain that Professor K. Skydsgaard expressed this very wish in his speech before the Pope at the audience for the observer delegates from the other Christian Churches:

> May I be permitted to refer here to something that seems to me to be very important? I am thinking of the part played by a scriptural theology which concentrates on the study of saving history in the Old and New Testaments. The more we advance in understanding of the mysterious and paradoxical history of the People of God, the more we begin really to understand the Church of Jesus Christ, both in her mystery and in her historical existence and her unity.

---

in 1954, the Marian Year, was Giovanni Battista Montini. Cf. H. Küng, *The Council and Reunion*, London, Sheed and Ward (1961), p. 185.

I hope Your Holiness will permit me to express our lively hope that the light of such a concrete, historical theology, that is, of a theology that draws its nourishment from the Bible and the Fathers, will shine more and more in the labours of the Council.

And it was not only a great joy for the observers but also a great encouragement to those Catholic theologians who have been working for years for such a theology when the Pope replied:

Your desire for the development of a "concrete, historical theology", which will "concentrate on saving history", is one that we for our part gladly endorse, and the suggestion seems to us to be one that deserves to be thoroughly explored. The Catholic Church already possesses institutions in which nothing would hinder stronger specialization in such studies; or indeed a new institute could be set up, if circumstances make it desirable.[1]

[1] *Herder-Korrespondenz*, 18 (1963-4), pp. 150-1.

5

IMPROVEMENTS IN CONCILIAR PROCEDURE

IT is very pleasant to have to report that the second session has seen the fulfilment of many of the improvements in the Council's procedure to which I referred in *The Living Church*, in the following points in particular:

(1) *Voting procedure*. It is no longer possible to swing the two-thirds majority by reversing the form of the question.[1] Acceptance of *schemata* still requires two-thirds. For rejection of a *schema* or adjournment of the discussion an absolute majority suffices. Even after the discussion, a minimum of fifty Fathers can submit general proposals or supplementary suggestions on a *schema*.

(2) *Latin*. It was announced that, on the initiative of Cardinal Cushing of Boston, who

---

[1] *The Living Church*, pt. 2, ch. 3.

once again left the Council early, a simultaneous translation system was to be set up.[1]

(3) *The Conciliar Secret*. This was practically abolished. It was maintained only as regards the texts of *schemata* and the work of the commissions. The Press complains more of an excess than a deficiency of information. Hence Press reports of the second session were significantly better than those of the first; there was no more chasing after rumours, and reporting was more objective, comprehensive and balanced. The members of the Council's Press office have done an important job outstanding well.[1]

(4) *Applause*. This is no longer forbidden in the *aula*. The minority, too, indicated their approval from time to time in this way.[1]

(5) *The work of the commissions*. Voting in the commissions has to be secret if at least five Fathers wish it. Three Fathers on a commission can call in a theological adviser who has not been called by the commission's president. This is meant to guard against the danger that one particular school of thought,

[1] *The Living Church*, pt. 2, ch. 3.

having the backing of the commission's officers, will simply impose itself. For the same reason, it is open to a majority of the commission to present its view to the *plenum* through its own chosen representative, thus avoiding the necessity of immediate recourse to some more or less satisfactory compromise. During this session, after many of the bishops had called for a radical reconstitution of the commissions and their presidents, the Pope ordered a new election of four new members to each (one more being nominated in each case by the Pope). At the same time the commissions were permitted to elect a second vice-president and secretary.

(6) *The Moderators.* The Pope appointed four moderators—Cardinals Agagianian (Curia), Döpfner (Munich), Lercaro (Bologna) and Suenens (Mechlin-Brussels)—of whom at least three (called "the Synoptics") represent the progressive majority of the Council. Their job is to lead the discussion in the General Congregations and to examine proposals submitted by the Fathers and pass them on to the appropriate commissions. Their most significant achievement was the vote on

the five questions (on episcopal consecration, collegiality and the diaconate), which they carried out against vigorous curial opposition.

(7) *The laity*. In the second session laymen were, for the first time, admitted as *auditores* —"hearers"; a merely token representation of the laity, because of their small numbers and passive role, but nevertheless a real representation. Their presence meant that, for the first time, Communion was distributed at the conciliar Mass each morning! On the last day but one of the session—at the ceremony commemorating the Council of Trent!—two of these laymen, the Frenchman Guitton and the Italian Veronese, were allowed not only to listen but to speak. The raising of these voices in the presence of the whole of this Church assembly, and of the Pope, was yet another symbol of an epoch-making change in the history of the Church. Great applause greeted Cardinal Suenens' proposal for (1) More of the laity at the Council; (2) Women (". . . unless I am mistaken, they make up half the human race"); (3) In particular, heads of women's religious orders. Thus the desired

goal of active participation by the laity in the Council slowly draws nearer.[1]

(8) *The Patriarchs.* The complaint of the Eastern Churches that their patriarchs, an institution going back to the earliest centuries of the Church, were given precedence only after the cardinals, a local Roman institution going back, in its present form, only to the Middle Ages, was accepted by Paul VI to the extent that the patriarchs are now no longer, as in the first session, placed beside and after the cardinals but occupy a position opposite to them.

[1] *The Living Church*, pt. 2, ch. 1.

6

THE DECISION ON LITURGICAL REFORM

THE one great, positive, definitive result of the second session is the final achievement of the Constitution on the Liturgy. At the beginning of the Council many voices had been raised against thorough renewal of the Liturgy, but at the final vote there were only four Noes against 2147 in favour. The Liturgical Commission did an endless amount of work, and did it well. The decree is epoch-making in its significance as regards the form taken by the worship of God; the age of the Council of Trent is over and a new thing is beginning.

The liturgical reform done by the Second Vatican Council to a great extent puts that done by the Council of Trent in the shade. This time, there is no question of a mere removal of abuses and re-establishment of the medieval *status quo*. What we have this time is, rather, a true return to the origins. This was only made possible by accurate knowledge of the development of the Liturgy, especially of the Roman Mass, down the centuries, as it has been worked out in the liturgical studies of the last few decades.[1] This provided a basis for creatively shaping a liturgy for the present day.

Of course this does not mean that what has been achieved is perfect. Much of it is even very disappointing. In the matter of the Breviary, one might, from the pastoral point of view, have expected an altogether more radical reform, penetrating through the monastic forms to the essential substance[2]; the chapter on the Divine Office can only to a very limited extent be said to have done this, especially as one thing that was not achieved was the integration of spiritual reading into the praying of the hours. Again, it is a crucial weakness in the reform of the Mass that it does not extend to the central problem, the renewal of the eucharistic prayer in the early Christian sense, without which it is not pos-

[1] Cf. *The Living Church*, pt. 3, chs. 1 and 5.
[2] *The Living Church*, pt. 3, ch. 5.

sible to give adequate expression to the scriptural "Do this in commemoration of me" and the proclamation, audible and intelligible, of the death of the Lord. [1 Cor. 11.26.] Is the reason for this that, whereas in liturgical studies very intensive work has been done on the historical development of the Mass, this has not, so far, been done on the basic scriptural data (the Supper as model and archetype of the Mass) and on the theology of the Eucharist? It is a pity, in any case, that during the preconciliar and conciliar discussions by experts the central question of the Canon was not discussed with sufficient frankness and thoroughness, partly out of excessive caution. A number of people are convinced that the overwhelming majority of the Council would have been prepared to go still further if the Commission—good though its work was—had led the way.

But these gaps, which, for the sake of the future, must not be passed over in silence, should not spoil our joy in the new constitution. It remains a great work. Consider the following points:

(1) The right principles for reform have been established throughout[1]; the right line of advance has been well laid down. Not only minor amendments but genuine structural reforms are envisaged. From the ecumenical point of view, the constitution represents a huge step forward in meeting those special concerns of Protestants which I outlined in *The Living Church*[2]: closer approximation of the Mass to the Supper of Jesus, a renewed hearing of the word of God intelligibly proclaimed, active worship by the whole priestly people, adaptation of the Liturgy to different peoples. As time goes on, the pastoral principles here laid down will manifest their power for good more and more.

(2) All controversial questions have been, in principle, decided in the sense of a positive renewal. This applies particularly to the old controversies between Catholics and Protestants: Communion under both kinds, concelebration, and above all the use of the people's language in the celebration of the

[1] *The Living Church*, pt. 5, ch. 3.
[2] pt. 3, ch. 4.

Eucharist.[1] All these things are not only not excluded; they are expressly permitted. In future, the chalice for the laity, concelebration and the people's language in the Liturgy will once again (!) exist in the Latin Church of the West—though initially with many restrictions. This means the elimination, in principle, of some important barriers to an ecumenical drawing-together in worship.

(3) Measures are included which can be immediately translated into action:

(a) As from the date of the constitution's coming into force, on 19 February 1964, a homily is obligatory at every Mass on Sundays; marriage is to be performed during Mass instead of before it; the Divine office can be recited in the mother tongue, with the permission of the bishop.

(b) It is the bishops' conference that is primarily to decide which texts of the Mass and the administration of the sacraments are to be in the mother tongue, what adaptations of the sacramental Liturgy are

[1] *The Living Church*, pt. 3, chs. 4 and 2.

to be made to various peoples, what form the new rite of marriage is to take etc.

(c) The Post-Conciliar Commission, which it is to be hoped will do its work both speedily and intensively, is to carry out a revision of all rites, which are to be simpler and more intelligible; a revision of the rite of Mass, so as to emphasize essentials and facilitate participation by the faithful; a revision of the Breviary, tightening it up, simplifying and shortening it; a new rite of concelebration; new cycles of readings from Scripture at Mass and in the Breviary; rules for Communion under both kinds; revision of the rites of baptism (both for children and for adults), of confirmation, penance, ordination and anointing of the sick; revision of the liturgical year, especially in regard to feasts of the saints; revision of the regulations about sacred buildings, vestments, liturgical vessels etc. The commission will thus have to decide about many valuable ideas contributed in speeches by the Council Fathers, as that the Canon should be modelled on Christ's Supper, that the words of consecration and

the doxology should be spoken aloud etc.
Hence many disappointed hopes may yet
be fulfilled by the Post-Conciliar Commission.

(4) There has been no closing of doors
against further developments in the spirit of
renewal. Rather, they have been explicitly
kept open, as the commission constantly re-
iterated (practically in connection with the
further introduction of the mother tongue).
Thus, for example, it is perfectly possible that
sooner or later some bishops' conference will
apply to Rome to have the whole Mass in the
mother tongue, which is ultimately the only
consistent and orderly solution. For all the
reasons now advanced for the celebration of
some parts in the mother tongue can certainly
be applied to the other parts as well; and here
let it be said once more: If there is one part
of the Mass that needs to be simplified, made
intelligible, and really *proclaimed*, then that
part is the eucharistic prayer, the Canon.
Much that seemed impossible five years ago
has become possible today. Much that sounds
unfamiliar today will be taken for granted in

five years' time. The only thing that matters is to go as resolutely and boldly on to the end of the road as the Council has resolutely and boldly set out on it. This is the task of the bishops' conferences and the Post-Conciliar Commission, but it is also the task of each individual parish, each individual parish priest and curate, each individual layman in the community of the Christian people.

7

THE REFORM OF ECCLESIASTICAL INSTITUTIONS

THE reform of the Liturgy is the heart of the whole, truly evangelical renewal of the Catholic Church that is going on today. But reform of the Liturgy is only the beginning, upon which other reforms have to follow. And it is here—not, indeed, in terms of definitive decisions, but of numerous concrete proposals—that the second session essentially surpassed the first.

The second point in the programme outlined in Pope Paul's opening speech did not merely stress the idea of *renewal within the Church* but presented it as springing from Christ and tending towards Christ:

> . . . renewal of the Church in our opinion, must follow from our awareness of the relationship by which Christ is united to his Church.

We have just spoken of the Bride of Christ looking upon Christ to discern in him her true likeness. If in doing so she were to discover some shadow, some defect, some stain upon her wedding garment, what should be her instinctive, courageous reaction? There can be no doubt that her primary duty would be to reform, correct and set herself aright in conformity with her divine model.[1]

It is only by following Christ that the Church can be credible in the eyes of the world:

To our way of thinking, this is the essential attitude, desired by Christ, which the Second Vatican Council must adopt.

It is only after this work of internal sanctification has been accomplished that the Church will be able to show herself to the whole world and say: "Who sees me, sees Christ", as Christ said of himself, "He who sees me sees also the Father." [John 14.9.]

In this sense the Council is to be a new spring, a reawakening of the mighty

[1] *Council Speeches*, p. 51.

spiritual and moral energies which at present lie dormant. The Council is evidence of a determination to bring about a rejuvenation both of the interior forces of the Church and of the regulations by which her canonical structure and liturgical forms are governed. The Council is striving to enhance in the Church that beauty of perfection and holiness which imitation of Christ and mystical union with him in the Holy Spirit can alone confer.[1]

Must it not arouse the attention of Protestant Christians, too, to hear how the Pope emphasizes the *Word of God* as the foundation for renewal of the Church, and calls for a *Church of love*?

May the living Church be conformed to the living Christ. If faith and charity are the principles of her life it is clear that no pains must be spared to make faith strong and joyful and to render Christian instruction and teaching methods more effective for the attaining of this vital end.

[1] *Council Speeches*, p. 51.

The first requirement of this reform will certainly be a more diligent study and a more intensive proclamation of the Word of God. Upon this foundation an education of love will be built up. We must give the place of honour to love and strive to construct the *Ecclesia caritatis* if we would have a Church capable of renewing herself and renewing the world around her. This indeed is a tremendous undertaking.[1]

The Pope praised the renewal of the Liturgy, saying: "Other fields will also receive the earnest attention of the Council Fathers."

The complex of problems connected with *the episcopate and the primacy* provided the first theme for reform on which, in close connection with the discussion of the *schema* on the Church, work was begun after the liturgical reform, in the discussion of the *schema* "On Bishops and the Government of Dioceses", from 5 November to 16 November. Not that this central problem was central to the *schema* itself. The reproach was, on the contrary, made against it that it had been

[1] *Council Speeches*, p. 52

worked out, largely behind the backs of the
Commission as a whole, on curial lines. Its
five chapters were on: (1) The relationship
of the bishops to the Roman Curia; (2)
Coadjutor bishops and suffragans; (3) National
bishops' conferences; (4) Boundaries of dioceses
and ecclesiastical provinces; (5) Erection of
parishes and their boundaries (this chapter
was not discussed, but passed on to the Commission for the Revision of Canon Law). The
discussion centred chiefly on those subjects
which are discussed in ch. 1, pt. 5, "The
Petrine Office and the Apostolic Office",
in *The Living Church*: decentralisation
(bishops' conferences) and representation of
the episcopate at the Church's centre (the
senate of bishops around the Pope), both pre-
supposing a radical reform of the Roman
Curia.

(1) *Reform of the Roman Curia*. Memories
were still vivid during the second session of
the fate of Father Riccardo Lombardi, who,
in a spirit of sheer loyalty to the Church, had
the audacity to voice some entirely objective
criticisms of the Roman Curia. But the
various forms of defamation and witch-hunt-

ing practised against those who put forward
informed and responsible proposals for dealing with this problem (one which is absolutely crucial for the renewal of the Church)
were checkmated on 21 September 1963 by
the Pope's sensational address to the Curia
itself.[1] Thus the second session was immediately preceded by an event which, again,
marks a turning-point in Church history: the
Pope himself took the loyal critics of the
Roman Curia under his protection and at
the same time put forward important proposals for reform.

The Pope was not sparing of praise for his
officials. And indeed, it is often the critics of
the Roman Curia who are more aware than
most of the amount of concrete work that it
accomplishes and of how much the Church
has owed, during recent centuries, to the
directive energy of its central organs. But the
Pope did not pass over the deficiencies of
the Curia, and he recognized criticism as
justified:

It is a summons to attention and obedience, an invitation to reform, a spur to

[1] *Herder-Korrespondenz*, 18 (1963–4), pp. 69–72.

perfection. We must receive the criticisms with which we are surrounded with humility and full consideration, and also with appreciation. Rome has no need to assume a defensive attitude while turning a deaf ear to suggestions made by honest voices, especially when these voices are the voices of friends and brothers. When accusations are, as they often are, unfounded, then it will answer and defend its reputation. But straightforwardly, without evasion or polemic. The world shall see that the efforts at present being made for a modernization of juridical structures and a deepening of spiritual awareness will not only encounter no resistance in the Roman Curia, the centre of the Church, but that the Curia itself will take the lead in that process of renewal which is constantly necessary in the Church as a human and earthly institution.

The demand for curial reform is brought out with full clarity:

It is easy to see that there are some reforms that need to be carried out in the

Roman Curia, and hence we must want to do them. As everyone knows, the latest reorganization of this ancient and complex organism goes back to the famous constitution *Immensa Aeterni Dei* of Pope Sixtus V in 1588. Pope St Pius X extended this reorganization by the constitution *Sapienti Consilio* in 1908. In this form it was incorporated, in essentials, into the Code of Canon Law in 1917. Many years have passed. It is understandable that such a structure should be suffering under the burden of its venerable age and feeling the lack of adaptation in its organs and practice to the needs and conditions of modern times, and at the same time the necessity for a simplification, a decentralization, a broadening, an adaptation to new tasks. So various reforms will be necessary. These reforms will be prudently weighed, so as to take account both of venerable and justified traditions on the one hand and of the needs of the age on the other. They will certainly be useful and beneficial in their effect, because they will have no other goal than to let go such forms and rules as are irrelevant and superfluous amongst those which guide the Curia, and to bring about whatever will make its competence better, more actual and more effective. These reforms will be formulated and promulgated by the Curia itself!

The Pope called for a decisive *international-ization* and *ecumenical formation* of the Curia:

Hence the Roman Curia will not, for example, have any fear of being organized according to broader, supra-national standards, nor of being penetrated by a better ecumenical formation. Did not St Bernard say, even in his time, "Why should not they be chosen from the entire world, who will one day have to judge the entire world?" [*De Consid.*, 4, 4.] So the Roman Curia will not ambitiously insist upon earthly privileges belonging to other days, nor on outward forms that are no longer appropriate for the emphasis and embodiment of true and lofty religious values. It will not fight to retain powers which can today, without any injury to the Church's universal order, be better exercised by the episcopate itself, on the spot. And never will scholarly aims and advances be made the subject of cautious or defensive action by organs of the Holy See, unless this is required for the sake of Church order and the salvation of souls.

With these bold words, and others that followed them, the Pope put himself at the head of those who are calling for a *reformatio* not only *in membris* but also *in capite*. He thus made himself the spokesman of all those bishops and countless others in the Church who have few things so much at heart as the reform of the Curia, on which so much depends for the Church and for the lasting success of the movement of renewal. The airing of this urgent question in the Council, in the presence of the whole episcopate, by voices coming from such various directions as those of Patriarch Maximos of Antioch, Cardinal Frings of Cologne, Archbishop De Souza of Bhopal, India, Bishop Méndez of Mexico, and others, is a fact of the first im-

4

portance, and has done the Church more good in the eyes of world opinion than any apologetic whitewash ever could.

It was demanded that the Papal Court, an institution of human, not divine, law, should not usurp the place of the college of bishops in the government of the universal Church; that episcopal titles should not be conferred *honoris causa* on the Curia; that curial officials should be the servants of the bishops, not their masters; that the Curia should not be dominated by one nation etc. But it was Cardinal Frings who touched the exposed nerve at the heart of the trouble when, in his quiet, balanced fashion, he attacked the practices of that least-beloved of all curial institutions, the Holy Office. The extent to which fear is still felt of this institution, founded at the beginning of the Counter-Reformation, is shown by the fact that only one bishop dared to speak these complaints aloud, though hundreds feel exactly the same. What Cardinal Frings criticized above all else was that the Holy Office stands above the law of the universal Church, insofar as its administrative and judicial acts are not bound by the provisions of the Code of Canon Law. Again, he criticized the practice of condemning works without any hearing being given to their authors or their immediate superiors. He demanded that the Holy Office should be subject to the Church's general law and that administrative and judicial proceedings should be clearly differentiated. Modes of procedure followed by the Holy Office no longer correspond to the present age and cause much anguish to souls and scandal to the world. He might have added that these modes of procedure also contradict various articles in the United Nations Declaration of Human Rights (10 December 1948), to which the Vatican is supposed to have given its assent (Article 10):

Everyone is entitled in full equality to a fair and public hearing by an independent and impartial tribunal, in the determination of his rights and obligations and of any criminal charge against him.

Article 11, 1:

Everyone charged with a penal offence has the right to be presumed innocent until

proved guilty according to law in a public
trial at which he has had all the guarantees
necessary for his defence.

Cardinal Frings' indictment was received
with applause in the *plenum* of the Council;
the Holy Office sought to defend itself by
angrily accusing the Cardinal of ignorance
and worse. The facts that the members of the
Holy Office are, with one exception, all of one
nation, that the consultors, though of different
nations, are all of one conservative line of
thought, and that the Pope, since his address
to the Curia, can even less than ever before be
simply identified with everything done by his
subordinate offices, are hardly disputable.
The necessity for a thorough reform of the
Holy Office was demonstrated *ad oculos* by
this incident, which was reported and un-
ambiguously commented on in the whole
world press. Unanimity of the subordinate
organs of the Holy See with the Pope himself
has not always been clear, either under John
XXIII or under Paul VI. This may be the
reason why Pope Paul, in his address to the
Curia, laid strong emphasis on curial obedience:

We are certain that no hesitations will ever emanate from the Curia in regard to the supreme will of the Pope, and that it will never be suspected that its mind and judgement are not in agreement with the mind and judgement of the Pope. If consent from the side of the Curia must always be strictly in accord [*rigorosamente univoca*] with what the Pope orders and desires, if this consent is indeed its law and its pride, then now is certainly the moment to acknowledge this firmly and publicly. . . . In any case, an understanding of this sort between the Pope and his Curia must remain the permanent, normal state of affairs, and not only exist and show its effects at the great moments of history. This understanding is always in order, for every papal decision, for this is befitting in regard to an organ immediately subject to him, which owes him absolute obedience; an organ of which the Pope makes use for the expression of his universal mission.

In other words, the Curia is at the disposal of the Pope, not the Pope at the disposal of the Curia.

The Council has not the slightest desire to impose on the Pope any reform of his own administrative machine. But the Fathers do want to present constructive proposals and desires to the Pope, who must obviously be deeply concerned to have the Church with him in this matter; they do want to stand at his side and assist him in this by no means easy task. For the Council, for renewal within the Church, and for the relation of the Catholic Church to the Christian world and the world at large during the coming decades, it is certainly going to be of crucial importance whether the Pope, with his far-seeing and truly Catholic ideas, succeeds in having his way with his own Curia, which has the same tendencies as any other administrative machine with a hierarchy of officials—tendencies towards autonomy, fossilization, perpetuation of past forms and functions, and retention and accumulation of powers.

(2) *A supreme senate for the Church.* In various speeches of the bishops the point was made that reform of the Curia would not be attained simply by taking some of their number into the Roman Congregations. It is

feared, not without reason, that a curialization of these bishops would result. What many cardinals and bishops from a great variety of countries and continents have asked for is rather a supreme senate of bishops, consisting so far as possible of representatives elected from time to time by the bishops' conferences and meeting periodically, several times a year, in Rome, so as to take counsel with the Pope and decide with him on the most important questions facing the Church: not another curial congregation over the other congregations but an episcopal college, independent of the Curia, with legislative power, together with the Pope, over the whole Church; this would bring out more clearly the character of the Roman Curia as a purely executive, subordinate, administrative organ.[1]

In this connection, too, the words of the Pope in his address to the Curia are significant:

It is a sacred rule for the officials of the Roman Curia to consult the bishops and avail themselves of their judgement in the

[1] Cf. *The Living Church*, pt. 5, ch. 1.

carrying out of their affairs. Among the consultors of the congregations there are not a few bishops who come from various regions. Indeed, we should like to go still further: If the Ecumenical Council should express the wish that, in harmony with the Church's teaching and with Canon Law, some representatives of the episcopate, especially from among the residential bishops, should be associated in a particular form and for particular tasks with the supreme head of the Church, then it certainly will not be the Roman Curia that will oppose this. It will rather see it as an increase in the honour and responsibility of its own lofty and irreplaceable service, which, apart from the necessary activities of the ecclesiastical tribunals in the Roman Curia and in the dioceses, is, as we well know, specifically of an administrative, advisory and executive nature.

With a supreme senate, the doctrine of the common collegiate responsibility and authority of the universal episcopate, together with the Pope, for the government of the whole Church, would not remain something purely theoretical. It would ensure that some degree at least of participation by the world episcopate in the government of the universal Church would take place in practice as well. Finally, it would guarantee a truly catholic representation at the centre of the Church not only of the different nations within her but of her different problems. It has been said that it is time that the Catholic Church, *mutatis mutandis*, should change from an Empire to a Commonwealth. What this means in relation to the Church's central government is this: the centralist, absolutist administrative and judicial structure of the Roman Curia, which has been described as the purest of all embodiments of eighteenth-century princely absolutism, is no longer suitable to the present age; it is in contradiction to a scripturally orientated ecclesiology and hence hinders the Church in the fulfilment of her task and in her service of Christendom and of the world. It is time for a form of Church government orientated rather to the apostolic Church in brotherly solidarity, which will involve the manifestation of a catholicity that is open to the special significance of the local and regional Church.

(3) *Bishops' conferences*. The idea of decentralization and the recognition of bishops' conferences has established itself throughout the Church. Even the very conservative *schema* on the bishops stresses the importance of the conferences. But a number of bishops spoke against the *schema*, because it speaks only of "granting powers" to the bishops. They point out with emphasis that the bishops *have* all the powers necessary for the government of their Churches, *iure divino*, by their consecration. So there should be no talk of "granting" powers, as though they belonged to the Pope alone, but rather of "restoring" powers which in themselves belong to the bishops. Consequently, what should be drawn up is not a list of the powers to be given back to the bishops but a list of the powers which the Pope, for the good of the whole Church, is to reserve to himself. A number of powers, admittedly not very important in character, for which the bishops have hitherto had to apply to Rome every five or twenty years, was in fact restored to them at the end of the second session by the Pope.

But it is perfectly clear to the bishops that

it is not possible simply to go back to the system in the early Church, when the individual bishop exercised considerable autonomy; and even then many decisions were taken not by individual bishops but by the episcopal synods. Rather than to the individual bishops, it is to the bishops' conferences that the important powers should be restored,[1] as has already been done in the Constitution on the Liturgy. The collegiality of the bishops needs to be realized not only at the universal, global level but also at the national and continental level, with proper attention to unity with the rest of the episcopate and with the Pope so as to avoid any harmful particularism. The essential collegiality of the episcopate, understood theologically and dogmatically, can indeed exist without the bishops' conferences, which are a pastoral institution of human law. The bishops' conferences are just *one* important, though territorially limited, manifestation of that essential, theological, dogmatic collegiality, a manifestation at the practical pastoral level. They are the expression not so

[1] Cf. *The Living Church*, pt. 5, ch. 1.

much of a juridical state of affairs as of communion in one mission and one service of the
one Church.

The controversial question that arises over
the bishops' conferences is whether their
decisions should be binding on individual
bishops or not. Two points emerge in the
discussion: One cannot have the bishops'
conference taking all initiative away from the
individual bishop; but on the other hand one
cannot have an individual bishop simply taking his own line in important questions affect-
ing the Church in his country or continent
when these are ones which require a common
unity. So presumably a middle way will be
found; decisions of the bishops' conference
will be binding on all bishops, but only where
questions of national or continental importance are concerned, and then only when there
is a pronounced majority of, say, two-thirds,
or even for some questions three-quarters. It
will be well here to aim only at a general
framework of rules, leaving it to individual
conferences to make adaptations to their own
special circumstances.

Those bishops' conferences which have

been functioning well for some time, such as the German and the French, show how much can be accomplished in this way by the Church of a particular country. There were, of course, further possible functions for the bishops' conferences brought forward at the Council, such as have not as yet been realized. Thus it was proposed, for instance,

(a) That the bishops' conferences should elect the bishops to be sent to the supreme senate;

(b) That the delegates of the bishops' conferences should, having proper regard to the universal Church, elect the Pope;

(c) That the bishops' conferences and their delegates should, in close co-operation with the Pope, take over the functions of the nunciatures.

Other questions in this *schema* were somewhat overshadowed by these three central questions of the Curia, the Senate and the bishops' conferences. However, besides the position of suffragan and coadjutor bishops, the following important problems were the ones specially discussed:

(1) *Age-limit for bishops*. This is a controversial question. Apart from pseudo-dogmatic reasons (the "mystical marriage" of a bishop with his diocese), the favourite argument brought against an age-limit of seventy-five is to cite great exceptions, which tend rather to prove the rule. Cardinal Suenens' speech showed impressively how urgent it is, given the speed of modern life, that we should not be content with mere exhortations in this matter; the development of a gulf between the bishop and his people, an ageing of the episcopate as a whole, are for various reasons more dangerous today than formerly. The episcopal office is meant to be a service of the People of God, from which a man retires when he can no longer perform this service with all the energy that it requires today.

(2) *The size of dioceses*. The very small Italian dioceses were attacked, but they also had defenders; and rightly so. One may well be of the opinion that if the bishop is really to carry out personally the tasks of preaching the Gospel, administering the sacraments, and caring pastorally for his people (as, for instance, the *schema* on the Church calls on him

to do), then dioceses have got to be small, and the bishop has got, at least to some extent, to know his people. The Italian system should not be criticized for having too small dioceses and too many bishops; it is rather the system in our countries that should be criticized, in which, because of the situation with which he is faced, the bishop can often be nothing more than an organizer and administrator. The small-diocese system is only wrong if each of its numerous bishops supposes anachronistically that he has to have his own curia and officials, his own matrimonial court, his own seminary, and so forth. These should be matters not for the bishops but for the metropolitans or archbishops, who should be reconstituted in their important function as real and effective (not merely formal, as under present canon law) intermediaries between dioceses (which would be smaller) and the central government of the Church in Rome: they would deal with the training of the next generation of priests, the pastoral care of bishops and clergy, ecclesiastical courts as needed etc. The bishops in our countries would all, by the standards of the early

Church, have to be called archbishops or metropolitans. The need, in this connection, to reconsider the question of the minister of confirmation also came out during the conciliar debate.

(3) *The diocesan council.* The principle of subsidiarity[1] was invoked in various connections during the second session. Obviously it does not only apply to the relation Pope–bishops, but also to the relation bishop–parish priest, and priest (clergy)–laity. Thus decentralization also needs to be carried out at the diocesan level. But on the other hand, collegiality also needs to be put into practice at the diocesan level. Just as in the course of time the idea of the college of bishops has faded and become almost forgotten, so also has the idea of the college of presbyters. Hence it was proposed during this session that there should also, at diocesan level, be a kind of senate around the bishop, to which the laity as well as clergy could belong.

But how much that had long been forgotten has now, through the Council, awakened

[1] Cf. *The Living Church*, pt. 5, ch. 1.

once again in the Church! Many of the problems that have arisen may cause discomfort to this or that person. But the Church does not live by being comfortable but by the Holy Spirit, who is driving men to renewal according to the will of God and the Gospel of Christ. Three years ago, the phrase *Ecclesia semper reformanda* was still, in the Catholic Church of the twentieth century, the programme of an isolated few. Today, it has not only become the Pope's own programme; he, indeed, spoke explicitly in his address to the Curia of "that permanent reform of which the Church, as a human and earthly institution, is always in need" ("Di quella perenne riforma, di cui la Chiesa stessa, in quanto istituzione umana e terrena, ha perpetuo bisogno"). More than this, *Ecclesia semper reformanda* has today become, in an unlooked-for way, a living reality. If there is one thing that has given people outside the Catholic Church a new positive interest in her, if there is one thing that has given people inside her a new joy in and love for the Church, it is this resolute will for reform and renewal according to the Gospel of Jesus Christ.

8

DIFFICULTIES

THE spirit of the second session was, if anything, better than that of the first, as I said in the introduction to this report. Who indeed could doubt it, looking back at everything that was said and done during this session? The Council, and everything that has been achieved in the Church in connection with the Council, has the look of an unexpected, undeserved miracle of the Holy Spirit. Yet it would be a mistake to think that the second session ended with morale as high as when it began. The sense of discomfort, which was widespread in many directions and abundantly reported in the Press, arose from the impression that the gap between the spirit of the Council and the definitive positive results it has achieved is too big. The standard applied to the second session in this respect was, rightly, different from that applied to the first. There has to come a time when the Council is no longer "playing itself in", a time when it gets down to producing serious results. The passing of the Constitution on the Liturgy, which had already been thoroughly discussed during the first session, seemed to many of the Fathers to be too meagre a result for the second. The decree on communications, passed all too hastily, without corrections or fresh discussion, has on the whole been an occasion for scepticism and criticism rather than praise; few expect it to have any serious influence on the course of events.

Would it really have been impossible to pass other *schemata*, besides that on the Liturgy, which, like it, had already been discussed during the first session? What are the reasons for this gap between the spirit of the second session and its definitive results? What are the reasons for the sense of discomfort that kept breaking through during the second session, even bringing to life again such essays as the first one in *The Living Church*,[1] resurrecting the fear that the movement of renewal, after getting off to so good a start,

[1] pt. 1, ch. 1.

might yet get bogged down precisely as did the movement for renewal in the late medieval councils before the Protestant Reformation? It is necessary and helpful to give, at least briefly, a calm and honestly objective analysis of the difficulties into which the Council has run, simply so as to seek out the ways along which it can make a better advance in the next session.

(1) *Direction of the Council*. The appointment of the moderators was generally hailed as a great step forward, and on the whole fully justified itself. The famous five votes showed that the moderators have the assembly with them when they take action in favour of a definite step forward for the Council and the achievement of some concrete results. Even the moderators, it is true, have had only limited success in speeding up the slow conciliar process and producing definitive results. But the criticisms levelled against them were unjustified to the extent that they had simply not been given the necessary powers to assert themselves, for instance, *vis-à-vis* the commissions. The inadequate basis and statement of the moderators' authority led, for instance, to

tiresome, wearying comings and goings over
the test votes, so that it was inevitable that
many of the Fathers should have their doubts
of any effective direction of the Council.
When it came to important decisions, the
three directing bodies—the moderators, the
Co-ordinating Commission and the Council
of Presidents—were liable to overlap and
paralyse each other. A clear ruling on who
is supposed to be effectively directing the
Council might be of decisive importance in
helping the third session on its way.

(2) *Procedure.* The improvements in procedure since the first session must not be overlooked. I have spoken of them already. But it
is still not possible simply to propose a motion
on a point of order and have it voted on
straight away. If the Fathers want to influence
the formal course of a debate, they are reduced
to manœuvrings and diplomacy behind the
scenes, with the outcome very uncertain. And
though simultaneous translation has been
decided on, the speeches still have to be made
in Latin, which effectively prevents spon-
taneous free discussion and the cutting down
or adaptation of speeches, at short notice, with

reference to the speeches that have gone before them. Nor does the point need stressing that it would be easier to find translators from one modern language into another than from scholastic Latin into modern languages. There are still too few speeches representing the bishops' conferences. One of the Italian bishops, who felt it incumbent on him to speak on practically every chapter of every *schema*, has perhaps in all twenty-eight diocesan priests under him; but he had to be given the same time and attention as the speaker for a bishops' conference representing perhaps a couple of thousand priests and thirty million Catholics. This means that the commissions—test votes on important questions having been the exception so far—cannot get any clear idea of the real mind of the *plenum*. During the debate on the vernacular, there were perhaps thirty bishops speaking against it and thirty in favour, but the latter had a round two thousand on their side; this only appeared later when it came to voting. It should also be observed that the time available each day for sessions is relatively short, sometimes, depending on the length of the

Liturgy, scarcely two and a half hours. It would be in accord with the new Liturgical Constitution to give up private masses during the coming session, to begin earlier, and celebrate the Eucharist in St Peter's in common (good planning would require only a short time for the communion of two thousand bishops; cf. the Eucharistic Congress at Munich, where there were several hundred thousand communicants).

(3) *Discrepancies between the Council and the commissions*. There are commissions which, though they have had their difficulties, have done outstandingly excellent work: the Liturgical Commission and the Secretariat for Unity. There are others of which the same cannot be said. The Theological Commission, though the *plenum* has devoted more time to its *schemata* than to any others, has so far not produced one single definitive result. Its *schema* on revelation was rejected; even the second version of it, worked out by a mixed commission, was still unsatisfactory and has so far not been presented. Its Marian *schema*, too, was, in the form in which it was presented, rejected. The first version of its

schema on the Church was sent back to the
Commission; the second version was still inadequate; one does not know what the third
will be like. Here, as in other commissions,
something more than technical deficiencies
is involved. It is asserted that several of the
commissions are working less in the spirit of
the Council than in the spirit of certain
circles in the Curia. The blame for this cannot be laid on their members, who, insofar as
they have been elected by the Council, are
working wholly in the spirit of the Council.
Towards the end of the second session their
numbers were strengthened by the Pope's
intervention. But there remains the problem
of the officers of the commissions. Unless it
can have commissions working completely
according to its spirit, the Council is to a large
extent blocked.

(4) *Resistance*. There is no need for everyone at the Council to have the same opinion.
Those who have long been members of the
progressive minority will be the last to desire
the suppression of the present (conservative)
minority. There may be and must be an
opposition. But an opposition must use the

right weapons when it fights; relevant arguments, constructive contributions to the discussion, and, finally and chiefly, the voting paper. But there are other things that are past understanding. For instance: that the president of a commission should present a *schema* which has not been approved by his commission; that the *Relator* of a commission should make a speech introducing a *schema* to the *plenum,* without having discussed it with his commission; that the printing and distribution of particular progressive *schemata* or chapters should be obstructed; that certain bishops should have difficulty in getting themselves placed on the list of speakers in time; that a bishop should have his freedom of speech restricted, when he has included in the summary of his speech (to be handed in three days in advance) the urgent problem of illegitimately married priests; that some *periti* should be rebuked for having, in a perfectly legitimate way, communicated papers to the bishops, while another can have his contribution printed at the Vatican Press and distributed in the *aula*; that a respected member of the presidential council, Cardinal

Frings, could, with impunity, be made the
target of a personal attack before the entire
plenum; that there should be an attempt, in
one commission, simply to set aside important
rules of conciliar procedure; that a massive
vote of the *plenum* of the Council, intended
as guidance for a commission, should with
impunity be publicly treated with contempt
by functioning presidents of commissions;
that further test votes, which could have
saved the commission a vast amount of unnecessary discussion, did not take place; that
sufficient time was not made available for
particular *schemata*, such as that on religious
liberty etc. I do not want to weary anybody.
The point is not the individual episode taken
in itself; this may have more than one interpretation. But could one keep quiet about all
this when enquiring into the reasons for the
sense of discomfort felt by so many of those
taking part in the Council? What is involved
is nothing more or less than the success of the
Council. Opposition can and should and must
be tolerated; but not obstruction.

(5) *The absence of exegesis.* Every morning, before the session begins, the Gospel is

solemnly borne to its place and enthroned:
the Gospel is to reign! In the debate on
revelation, as in that on the Liturgy and that
on the Church, there have been innumerable references to the fundamental importance of referring everything to Holy Scripture.
Yet—and in the current state of biblical
studies and biblical renewal in the Catholic
Church, this is more than mere chance—
working exegetes are not playing any part
worth mentioning in the Council. In com-
parison with the great number of systematic
theologians and canonists they simply do not
count. Is it chance that neither the Pontifical
Biblical Institute at Rome nor the École
biblique at Jerusalem has been integrated
into the work of the Council? Of the German
Catholic New-Testament scholars of the front
rank, men who, in this age of ecumenism,
know Protestant exegesis not merely from far
off but intimately, not one is present at the
Council: neither Kuss nor Schelkle nor
Schlier nor Schnackenburg nor Vögtle. . . .
Obviously, exegesis cannot be neglected with
impunity. Many of the problems, for instance,
that came up in the discussion on the Church

had been inadequately worked out in terms of exegesis (and of the history of dogma). Many questions which absolutely needed to be raised (such as the charismatic structure of the Pauline communities, the development of office in the New Testament etc.) were not raised at all. Yet what a gain it would be to the *schema* on the Church if Scripture were not merely "quoted" in it (and even its Scripture quotations were often criticized in the discussion as inaccurate), but the whole *schema*, with the help of an appropriately large number of exegetes (nothing less would suffice to carry the point in the commission), were given a shape springing entirely from the New Testament. The same applies to other *schemata*; practical, pastoral decrees too could make use of exegesis, for these too need to be tested by Scripture. If exegetes began to take a proportionate share in the Council, much doubt and discomfort would be brought to an end amongst the theologians themselves. They could give the Council an unlooked-for positive impulse.

It is time to stop. This realistic enumeration of the many difficulties at work is not to be misunderstood. They were not brought forward as criticism for criticism's sake. They have not been listed to obscure all the positive elements, with which the greater part of this report has been concerned. The point of enumerating them was to recall the memory of all those positive things in, as it were, the light of the negative ones; to remind us, that is to say, how much is at stake. It remains, as before, a question of the success or failure of the Council.

9

THE SUCCESS OF THE SECOND
SESSION, AND THE THIRD

As before, there is no ground for pessimism, but much for thought and still more for hope. The spirit of renewal, as we have encountered it throughout this report, is strong enough to overcome all difficulties and all resistance. They need only to be clearly envisaged and energetically tackled. How difficult the situation was before the first session, and how quickly it changed! We have constantly had this experience at the Council; whenever the Council ran into particularly serious difficulties, there came an increase of energies to overcome them.

It is difficult to pass any final judgement on the second session. So many questions remain open. Before the end of the session, Cardinal Bea said that postponement did not mean shelving. True, postponement can be a bad thing, but it can also be good. It allows time for growing used to new things which are often, in fact, so very old; for becoming clear about the reasons for things; for examining difficulties; for taking note of the beneficial effect in the Church and the world of what has already been announced etc. This was how it was with the liturgical *schema*: much that seemed dubious at the end of the first session had become obvious by the beginning of the second. Why should it be any different this time? The third session will no longer be able to avoid the decisions which were, in so many cases, postponed in the second. The third session will decide the success of the second.

What will decide the success of the third session and of the Council as a whole is whether the Gospel of Jesus Christ is taken seriously. May the Pope's pilgrimage to Jerusalem be understood as what it was meant to be: a return to the origins, a return to Jesus, and for this very reason an encounter with our brothers: Christians, Jews, Moslems and the whole world.

10

THE COUNCIL—END OR
BEGINNING

THE fourth session of the Second Vatican Council—and, it is said, the last—has already been called for September 14th, 1965. The opinions as to the value of its achievements so far, however, are very mixed, not only outside the Council, but also within it. In order to make an examination which combines critical sobriety with sympathetic understanding, there is no better question to be put than this: Why such differences in the opinions, differences which run the entire gamut from dejected pessimism to unbridled optimism? This question makes us aware of several formal criteria which are not only capable of explaining the differences among the expressed opinions concerning the Council, but also bring to light the inner tensions of the Council itself.

THEORETICAL CONCLUSIONS—PRACTICALLY IMPLEMENTED?

Varying judgements about the Council will result depending on whether one looks at theoretical conclusions or practical effects. The theoretician as well as the pragmatist can do both.

One who is primarily interested in theoretical conclusions will welcome—for example—the establishment of a common, collegial direction of the Church by pope and bishops as a decisive counterpoint to the First Vatican Council's one-sided definition of papal supremacy. One who is primarily interested in practical effects will agree with this, but at the same time will want it to be borne in mind that this decree concerning collegiality has, as a matter of fact, not yet changed anything in Rome itself.

The first will point to the fact that, beyond a merely theoretical collegiality, an international episcopal council (senate) will be decided upon by the Council—a senate which is to be set over the Roman Curia in everything. The second will say that everything

5

depends upon the manner in which this decree is implemented; whether the members of this council will be elected freely by the national or regional bishops' conferences or whether—like the College of Cardinals—they will be appointed by the Pope; whether its actual authority will be great or small, etc.

The first will be happy that the Council, relating itself to the Gospel in a new way, understands the Church as a Church in the service of the poor. The second will ask—in consideration of the simple papal liturgy at the beginning of the third session, which, however, soon again became a Baroque liturgy in the old style—whether anything at all has been done until now either by the Council or by any of the bishops' conferences to live up to the resolution in practice, by giving up all unevangelical pomp and ostentation in vestments, ornamentation, titles, displays of honour.

The first will call the Council's espousal of religious liberty a milestone in the history of the Church, which indicates a new phase of genuine tolerance for many Catholic countries. The second will only be satisfied by an approved conciliar declaration and actions which testify for freedom not only outside the Catholic Church, but also within, and he will therefore await the abolition of the Index, censorship and inquisitorial methods.

The first will praise the fundamental reform of the Liturgy which was adopted a year ago as a commitment to a simpler, intelligible, evangelical liturgy. The second will point to the fact that in many bishops' conferences as well as in Rome the implementing of the reform takes place with little enthusiasm and with exceptional hesitation, casuistry and inconsistency.

In short: Whoever is interested in the first place in theoretical conclusions will find sufficient ground for a victorious optimism; whoever is primarily concerned with practical consequences, for a disheartened pessimism.

ECCLESIASTICAL OR ECUMENICAL PERSPECTIVE?

Again, a variety of opinions will be obtained depending on whether one sees the Council from within the Catholic Church or from an ecumenical viewpoint (or from the viewpoint of the "modern world"). This is not dependent upon whether the observer is Catholic or non-Catholic. The Catholic, too, can assume an ecumenical viewpoint by appealing to the fact that John XXIII, as well as Paul VI, gave the Council an objective which was not merely Catholic, but also ecumenical. On the other hand, the non-Catholic Christian, or even the non-Christian can—in order to form an opinion of the Council—assume a Catholic viewpoint, giving as his reason that one can judge a Catholic Council justly only from within. The significance of this formal criterion is easily illustrated with reference to the constitution "On Revelation" which will be promulgated at the next session, and to the constitution "On the Church" which has already been promulgated.

In relation to the constitution "On Revelation", the observer who evaluates it from the Catholic viewpoint will emphasize that Vatican II's understanding of revelation is much less rationalistic than that of Vatican I and that the centre of the dispute—i.e., whether everything definitive for revelation is contained in the Holy Scriptures—has, in any case, not been decided negatively. The observer who evaluates the constitution from the ecumenical viewpoint will regard precisely this inconclusive treatment of the question of the relationship of Scripture and Tradition as the principal fault of the constitution and at the same time feel the lack of a better statement of the relationship between "natural revelation" and "historical revelation", as well as a treatment of the question of the "natural" knowledge of God.

The first will hail the full affirmation of the historical-critical method of exegesis (*re* literary *genres*, literal sense, etc.) which takes seriously the humanity and frailty of the written word, as a victory for modern exegesis over the reactionary tendencies which came to light in Rome even during the reign of John XXIII, tendencies which the encyclical *Divino Afflante Spiritu* was intended to reverse. The second will observe that the description of biblical inspiration takes not the slightest notice of the results of modern exegesis and historical research and that consequently, in spite of the fact that today secular, scientific and historical errors can easily be established, no attention has been paid to "total inerrancy" of the Scriptures.

The first will commend the emphasis placed upon the importance of the Old Testament for the New, the rejection of a dogmatic prejudging of historical questions (authorship of the books of the Bible, among others), and the prominence given to the significance of the oral proclamation and tradition, to the kerygmatic character of the Gospels and to *Formgeschichte*. The second will say that for any well-informed theologian the expressions used in this particular chapter—like so many in this constitution—are obvious and even, to some extent, trite, and that three years' exertion in the Council was hardly necessary in order to come up with such formulations.

The first will regard the last chapter on the Scriptures in the life of the Church as a high point in this constitution, because here the unique significance of the Bible for the Church is brought to light as never before in an official Catholic document, the Bible is defined as the norm for preaching, theology and the Church, and good translations of the Bible from the original texts are encouraged (where possible, together with other Christians!) as well as private Bible reading. The second will admit all this, but at the same time ask whether there is not a conspicuous contradiction between this chapter and the other on Scripture and Tradition, which, appealing to Trent, goes a long way towards placing both of these great concepts on the same level.

In relation to the constitution "On the Church", the observer who evaluates it from the Catholic viewpoint will find an image of the Church revealed which is both more balanced (not simply concentrated on "the Body of Christ") and more biblical; he will see the Church characterized as on pilgrimage rather than in triumph and for the first time he will ascertain a difference between the Church of Christ and the visible Roman Catholic Church. The one who evaluates the document from the ecumenical viewpoint will say, in spite of all the indisputable progress, that it is to be noted throughout the decree that the exegetes had no decisive say in it and that a quite different and convincing image of the Church could have been sketched on the basis of contemporary exegesis.

The first will see an uncommonly fruitful starting-point in the understanding of the Church as the People of God, from which the common priesthood of the laity could be more easily made evident through the notion of the clerical order as an order of service; he will characterize as great progress the further point that the charisms of the individual Christian are stressed and also the particular Churches of the individual dioceses and nations and, at the same time, Churches and ecclesiastical communities outside the Catholic Church are expressly recognized, as well as the possibility of salvation for non-Christians. The second will reply to this, however, in all fairness and truth, that the common priesthood of the laity is not thought through to its logical conclusion, that the charismatic structure of the Church is not understood as such, that the presentation of the sacraments is theologically inadequate and the expressions concerning the *sensus fidelium* and the infallibility of the Church are open to misunderstanding.

The first will conclude with great satisfaction that just as Peter, together with the Apostles, was charged with the chief guidance of the Church, so also is the Pope together with the bishops; that the understanding of ecclesiastical office is not power but service, that the importance of the local church has been established, as well as the reintroduction of the diaconate even for married men. The second will consider thoroughly unclear exegetically, historically and systematically, the concept of "apostle" (apostle = "the Twelve"?), the question of the apostolic succession of the bishops, the relationship of bishops and priests, as well as the concepts "sacrament", "sacramental character", etc.; he will find the difference between divine and human law not clearly thought through (the summoning of councils by the Pope, the three levels of the Hierarchy, the case of conflict between Pope and Church, etc.) and will feel the lack of any mention of the partial nature of all ecclesiastical doctrinal formulations in the statement on ecclesiastical infallibility.

The remaining chapters of the constitution on the Church could be gone through in the same way: on the vocation of all to sanctity, on religious, the eschatalogical character of the church and especially the chapter on Mary, where the first will praise the renunciation of further Marialogical dogma, while the second will find fault with a mariology which continues to be unclear exegetically and historically and which, for other Christians, is —although moderate—still out of proportion. In short: In the other constitutions and decrees, just as in both of these constitutions, the observer who evaluates the Council from within the Catholic Church will find sufficient grounds for good cheer, the one who evaluates from the ecumenical viewpoint, for dejection.

PROVISIONAL OR RADICAL SOLUTIONS?

One's opinion on the Council will once again be quite different, depending upon whether one tended at the outset toward provisional solutions or radical ones, whether one reckoned on dealing tactically and prag-

matically with the political possibilities or
was, on essentially theological grounds, concerned with objective accuracy. It is, of
course, possible in this case also for an ecclesiastical politician to assume a fundamentally
theological viewpoint and—vice versa—for
a theologian to assume a tactical-political
one.

The tactical and pragmatic thinker will not
be able to praise enough the restoration of a
genuine liturgy of the word and the limited
introduction of the vernacular in divine
service. The essentially theological thinker
will reply, however, that the reform of the
Liturgy has not, as yet, dared to tackle what is
really crucial, namely, the reform of the
Canon of the Mass and the restoration of the
ancient eucharistic prayer, that the linguistic
hodgepodge in the Mass is a sign of inconsistency, that the retention of Latin precisely for
the central and most important parts of the
eucharistic celebration is certainly most
incomprehensible.

The first will praise the theological as well
as practical affirmation of the collegiality of
pope and bishops as the main accomplish-

ment of Vatican II. The second will say that collegiality is a characteristic of the Church as such (as the community of the faithful and the People of God) and that, therefore, not only is the collegiality of the Pope with the bishops to be taken seriously, but also that of the bishops with pastors, and that of pastors with parishioners.

The first will emphasize the exceptionally understanding voices which were raised in the *aula* on the delicate question of birth control. The second will expect more than negative condemnation of some aspects of this question be avoided, while an ambiguous silence is preserved with regard to the rest; he will expect that a constructive answer should be given, and, if necessary, previous errors calmly admitted.

In this way, finally, the practical-political thinker will also find grounds for optimism, the essentially theological thinker for pessimism.

And in order to make quite clear how very difficult it is to form an opinion of the Council, at least at the moment of writing, it should be taken into consideration that

among the six different viewpoints given, the
widest variety of combinations is possible:
that the person who is of a primarily theoretical orientation as well as the one who is of
a primarily practical orientation, could be
either ecumenically or ecclesiastically orientated, either tactical-political or essentially
theological, etc. Should one still have the
courage, in the face of this, to offer an opinion
as to the achievements of the Council thus
far?

UNFOUNDED OR WELL-FOUNDED HOPE?

It would, in any case, be too complicated,
and yet too simple, to arrive at one's own
opinion by some combination of the pro-
ferred possibilities. Too complicated because
the positive and negative elements do not
permit themselves to be simply added together; too simple, because it presumes that
an exclusive choice—of either the first or
second viewpoint—would be adequate to
express the concrete reality. One need only
consider that the exclusive choice of the
first series (theoretical—ecclesiastical—pro-

visional) leads necessarily to a totally decep-
tive optimism and, on the other hand, the
exclusive choice of the second series (practical
—ecumenical—radical) leads necessarily to
abysmal pessimism. The first would come to
the conclusion that the Council could not
possibly have done any better, although, in
reality, the deficiencies are notorious and the
unfulfilled aspirations innumerable. The
second would come to the conclusion that it
has hardly been worthwhile to have a Council, although, in reality, the shift to the positive is manifest and the achievement so far
immeasurable.

The truth, accordingly, does not lie some-
where in the middle, as though one could
produce an easy synthesis by means of a con-
veniently harmonious this-as-well-as-that. The
concern here is not for a proper synthesis of
viewpoints, but for a genuine dialetic in historical dynamism. In other words, the first
term in our disjunction tends towards the
second; or, to put it less condensedly, *the
theoretical conclusions cry out for practical
consequences; progress within the Catholic
Church bears—indirectly and often quite*

directly—ecumenical fruit; the provisional and tactical solutions are both the inception of and the demand for radical and fundamental solutions.

All of this, certainly, will not come about of itself. Much can be lost by indolence, cowardice and indecision; much can be blocked by intrigue, obstructionism and brute use of power. And the difficulties which plague this Council day by day ought not to be belittled. Among them, and not the worst, by far—despite what one hears—is that there is too much talk, debate, even mere chatter, in the Council and too few decisions. The greatest hindrance since the beginning of the Council—and this has become clear in the last weeks of the third session to even the most naïve—is the fundamental antagonism which has become evident in all things, not so much between the majority of the Council and a minority, as between the Council and a group of the Curia, which, although small in number and without any backing from the faithful, is exceptionally powerful in that it finds itself in possession not only of the most important key positions of the Curia (Roman

Congregations) but also of the Council itself; this group places presidents, numerous vice-presidents and secretaries of most of the conciliar commissions as well as the all-too-powerful general Secretariat of the Council. How different many things would have been by the end of the third session, how different many things would have been right from the beginning of the Council, had only the commissions not been under the control of the Curia! In the Curia rather than directly in the Council lies the chief reason that numerous words and deeds of the Council have appeared to many to be ambiguous compromises rather than clear decisions; the reason why numerous words have been followed by no deeds. Is the entire Council, then, an empty hope? In an objective realism which combines critical sobriety with sympathetic understanding, it is possible to say with caution: Despite all of the great difficulties and serious limitations, there is an ever more thoroughly grounded hope! Why? A few instances may suffice to show that the Council, despite all opposition, is on the right track (we shall return to this point)—provided that it is neither decisively hindered nor blocked on its way:

(1) *No doors were closed*: One ought not to take this for granted. The schemata of the preparatory commission were full of condemnations, even if formulated without the earlier usual anathema. The Council, however, has declined to settle any important questions in a decisively negative way. What a difference from the Catholic Church of earlier centuries, even from the Catholic Church of the first half of this century (one remembers the encyclical *Humani Generis* of 1950)! Significantly, there has been an abstention from all positive, as well as negative, definitions and formulations of dogma. Unlike Vatican I, the Second Vatican Council is persuaded that the appeal to an ecclesiastical infallibility is not sufficient to answer the complex theoretical as well as practical questions of the contemporary Church and mankind. In the background is the conviction that many earlier definitions could be more hindrance than help for the present-day Church in the encounter with other Christian Churches and with the modern world. The

increasingly apparent post-conciliar defensive position of certain curial circles over against episcopal collegiality—namely, that in regard to collegiality and other subjects there is no concern for final definitions—must not tempt the progressive majority of the Council to insist upon definitions. The truth will prevail just as well without definitions.

(2) *Innumerable doors were opened*: One need merely imagine oneself once again in the period just before the first session of the Council; what courage was required of the few who dared to raise certain questions for discussion, how many kept quiet at that time through either fear or resignation, how many were of the opinion that nothing at all could come of this conciliar enterprise . . . We have already become spoiled! There is not a single question (birth control and celibacy not excluded) which cannot be discussed in the Catholic Church today. Principles such as "Ecclesia semper reformanda", which many Catholics considered arch-Protestant in 1960, are found now in the decrees of the Council.

(3) *A new spirit has been brought to life*: The letter can remain dead. Discussion can

run out, decrees can be watered down and forgotten. It is decisive whether a new spirit has quickened the letter. It is indisputable that a new spirit—a spirit of renewal and reform, of ecumenical understanding and of dialogue with the modern world—has taken hold of the bishops and theologians of the Council and, together with them, the whole Catholic Church. This spirit is so powerful that the decrees are, basically, always limping along behind what has already been brought to life in the Church through it. An intelligent interpretation of a decree, accordingly, will not be snagged by the terms of the decree, which are often the result of a compromise, but—plainly in agreement with earlier versions of the same decree—will look to the underlying spirit of renewal and reform which is decisive for the future.

(4) *Substantial positive results have been achieved*: When one recalls the expectations held before the beginning of the Council, which have been described by many as excessive, one may conclude that the Council has not done badly up until now; on the contrary, rather well. The reform of the Liturgy alone,

which was decided upon at the end of the second session and which will prevail in the Church against all delaying tactics, would have made a Council worthwhile. And in the third session another three important constitutions were ratified: the constitutions on the Church, on ecumenism and on the Eastern Churches. Whatever was not finally ratified in this session can be ratified in the fourth session. Certainly a great deal is unsatisfactory; and I do not want to withdraw anything of what I said at the beginning of this section. Every one of these documents contains, however, innumerable openings and initiatives which open new ways and a new future. That can be briefly illustrated by a simple enumeration of a few key themes of the constitution "On Ecumenism": blame on both sides for schism, and the request for pardon by other Christians; the Catholic Church as a church of sinners needs constant reform not only in practical church life, but also in doctrine; the Gospel as norm for renewal; non-Catholic Christian communities also called "Churches" or "ecclesiastical communities"; the necessity of an ecumenical attitude, improvement of the knowledge of one another on both sides, dialogue, recognition of the good existing among others, learning from them, co-operation in all areas, common prayer with separated Christians.

THE SETBACK

It has always been made clear in innumerable Press reports that the Roman Curia or, rather, certain powerful circles in it, are the actual centre of the resistance to a renewal of the Catholic Church and an encounter with the other Christians and the modern world. This has always been the reason for much of the scepticism in regard to the Council. In this regard it needs to be repeated with emphasis: The opposition is only secondarily an opposition between a progressive majority of the Council and a conservative minority. The opposition is primarily that between the progressive Council itself and the reactionary Curia. If only those bishops had a seat in Council who—as residential bishops or auxiliaries—have a diocese (i.e., the faithful) behind them, and were all of the Curia's "honorary bishops", who have no more than a very powerful ecclesiastical bureaucracy behind them, excluded from the Council, from its direction and commissions, the reactionary minority—according to experience and the voting results in most cases so far—would have dwindled to a few outsiders with no influence. Because the situation is, as a matter of fact, the opposite and the Curia controls—not completely, but to a very great extent—the conciliar apparatus and means of doing business, these painful incidents were able to take place which in the last two weeks of the third session upset the Council and have been taken in the world at large as a set-back for the Council and the constructive goal set for it. It was not that the well-known obstructionism of the Curia was regarded as of primary importance; rather, the fact that the larger part of the bishops, theologians and non-Catholic observers had the fatal impression that the Pope—for whatever reason, be it fear, or theological uncertainty, or concern for his immediate surroundings and Italian domestic policy—had put himself behind the obstructions and manoeuvring of the Curia.

The development of the conciliar crisis does not have to be recited here in detail:

1. The intrigue against the statement on the Jews;

2. The commitment of the Pope to a missions schema which had been worked out completely under the supervision of the Roman Congregation for Missions and which was afterwards rejected by the Pope and a great majority of the bishops as thoroughly inadequate;

3. The *nota explicativa* watering down the concept of collegiality, which was forced upon the Council without ever being submitted to a vote;

4. The last-minute changes ordered by the Pope in the schema "On Ecumenism", changes which were less friendly to non-Catholics and which had been given only nominal approval by the Secretariat for Unity;

5. The reference of the disputed questions of marriage morality and mixed marriages to the Pope, or rather to curial commissions;

6. The further postponement, pushed through on formal grounds in spite of a mas-

sive protest from well over one thousand
bishops, of the statement on religious liberty,
which has now been held back for three
Council sessions and which is awaited by the
entire world with impatience—a postponement which was approved by the Pope;

7. The promulgation of the misleading
title *Mater Ecclesiae* against the expressed
will of the Council majority, which will
arouse in non-Catholic Christendom great
indignation, and grave doubts as to the
genuinely ecumenical sympathies of the
Pope;

8. The lack of that support which Pope
Paul VI had given to the Council, up to the
middle of the second session, as well as the
change of tone from his grand opening
speech.

Would it be wise, or honourable or useful
in this situation, which has found a very
critical response in the entire world press, if
one kept silent within the Church concerning
what all the newspapers are full of; that the
prestige—no, the credit—of the Pope has
received a powerful blow which his reception
in India, no matter how triumphal, cannot

make up for, and that confidence in the Pope, which, in the days of John XXIII, had reached a hitherto unknown height, has appeared to many both inside and outside the Catholic Church to have sunk to zero? It would be too sad to report here all the bitter words and reactions which I heard from so many well-intentioned people while on a lecture tour round the world at the end of November and beginning of December, 1964. So great a number of newspaper articles and the much-read book of "Michael Serafian", *The Pilgrim*, cannot be refuted by an apologetic which passes by the real issue, but only by deeds, namely, by deeds of Pope Paul VI himself.

Certainly, everyone knows that the situation in Curia and Council is complex and every deed or absence of deed on Pope Paul VI's part can be interpreted, on the most various grounds, as for or against either this or that. No-one questions the Pope's good will. People hope, however, both inside and outside the Church, for a rapid fulfilment of what the Pope himself has solemnly promised to the Church and the world: a serious, radical reform of the Roman Curia, including structures as well as persons. To put it concretely:

1. Internationalization of the Roman Curia;

2. The creation of an episcopal senate, placed over the Curia, convening periodically in Rome, which works out, together with the Pope, the decisive directives for the guidance of the Church;

3. Decentralization of the power of the Curia in relation to the Bishops' Conferences.

The Council not only stands completely behind this programme; it has laid the groundwork for it, especially in the schema on the pastoral responsibility of the bishops, which, contrary to expectations, could not be promulgated. In any case, there is widespread fear among the bishops that the decisions in question will remain as dead letters in that the Pope as well as the Council was only partially successful in pushing them through even during the session, and in that the efforts of the Curia are well known; namely, on the one hand, to interpret what has already been decided in a minimizing way and to limit its implementation as far as possible;

and, on the other hand, to reconquer the old positions quickly and decisively in accordance with the well-known Roman saying, "The councils pass away, the popes pass away, but the Curia Romana goes on forever!" Will it be possible to limit this bureaucratic apparatus, with its wealth of traditions and stratagems, which is for various reasons, considered to have little love for the present Pope as well as the Council, to those functions proper to it in its service of the Church, so that one day the Catholic Church will evolve from Roman Empire into Catholic Commonwealth? *Everything will depend upon whether the indisputable setback to the Council and the loss of confidence in the Pope will be compensated for by the courageous, energetic and resolute action of the bishops together with the Pope, action which will not shrink from exerting legitimate pressure in those places where only pressure can help effectively.* Even a few changes of personnel in the Curia and Council could be a sign to the Church and the world that a small power group will not succeed in dominating Council and Pope—a group which,

although certainly in good faith, is unfortu-
nately backward-looking, ghetto-bound and
unecumenical, both traditionalist and nation-
alist in its thinking, which identifies itself
with "the Church" and would "excommuni-
cate" everyone who thinks otherwise. The
fourth session will show whether the Council,
which has won so many battles, will also win
the war in the end. There are still enough
important themes remaining in the Council's
order of business: renewed discussion of the
schema "The Church in the Modern World",
religious liberty, the missions, the priesthood;
further, the votes on the schemata on revelation and on the lay apostolate as well as votes
relative to the improvement of the schemata
on the pastoral responsibility of the bishops,
religious, the seminaries, the Christian training of children, the relationship of the
Church with the Jews and the non-Christian
religions. Whether the Council can be com-
pleted with the fourth session is questionable.
After the third session, many a bishop, asked
whether he considered three more Council
sessions or an earnest reform of the Curia
(episcopal senate, internationalization, decen-

tralization) to be more important, would name the reform of the Curia, without any hesitation.

A STANDSTILL IS NO LONGER POSSIBLE

The movements which have been released by the Council in the Catholic Church have reached such a depth and breadth that they will follow their own inherent legitimacy. Every impulse releases other impulses. Every movement in a sector of the Church's life means indirectly a movement in some other sector. It cannot be anticipated how one will follow another. Each act of reform has its own consequences. Through the Council, the Catholic Church has entered into a hopeful transitional phase full of new life and unforeseen movements, so that the problem of order and obedience has presented itself in a new way to both laity and clergy. What should be thought of the pastor or assistant or layman who is more obedient to the impulses of the Council than, perhaps, his own bishop? Obedience—subject to the will of God—is to be expected of everyone in the Church. And the greater the responsibility the greater the obligation to obedience. At a time when so much has happily been set in motion in the Church, it is precisely the cleric who puts himself resolutely and courageously in the forefront and who is not especially content to function as a brake, who provides best for order in freedom in his own province. That is the great hope of the Council. The Council does not stand alone, it has the entire Church behind it and it will be borne along by the entire Church. This Church, which is itself greater and stronger than the Council, wants to go further and will go further. Even if the movements which have been set free in the Catholic Church by John XXIII and the Council should be artificially braked, they would not permit themselves to be stopped. This would lead, however, to the most highly dangerous tensions, concerning which one can do no more than give a warning at present, and to an extremely serious crisis of confidence in regard to ecclesiastical office, which will not result in a new schism (no-one today would find that worth the trouble), but rather in a further quiet exodus from the

Church on the part of so many for whom the Council has rekindled a new hope for a renewed Church and a unified Christendom. And who should like to take upon himself the responsibility for that?

Is it necessary, after all that has been said, to explain why this section was given the title, "The Council—End or Beginning?" Four hundred years ago, the small and outwardly unpretentious Council of Trent could introduce—with its limited means and with its often negative, merely restorative objectives—an entirely new epoch of church history in spite of indescribable difficulties. Should not the Second Vatican Council, in spite of all the indisputable difficulties, but with completely different means and possibilities and completely different positive and constructive objectives, have the power to do this just as well—even much better? The post-tridentine epoch of the Counter-Reformation has finally ended for the Catholic Church. The hitherto unfulfilled reform of the Roman Curia may not be used as the basis of an excuse to put off *the manifold necessary renewal at every level of the parish, and the diocese, and of ecclesiastical office.* Concrete tasks are not lacking even outside of Rome! It is a grace and a task, a hope and a challenge, when we say: The Council—not an end, but a beginning!

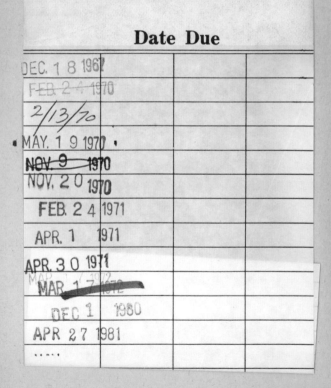

Date Due

DEC. 1 8 1967		
FEB 2 4 1970		
2/13/70		
MAY. 1 9 1970		
NOV. 9 1970		
NOV. 2 0 1970		
FEB. 2 4 1971		
APR. 1 1971		
APR. 3 0 1971		
MAR 1 7 1972		
DEC 1 1980		
APR 2 7 1981		
. . . . .		